Rx from the Garden

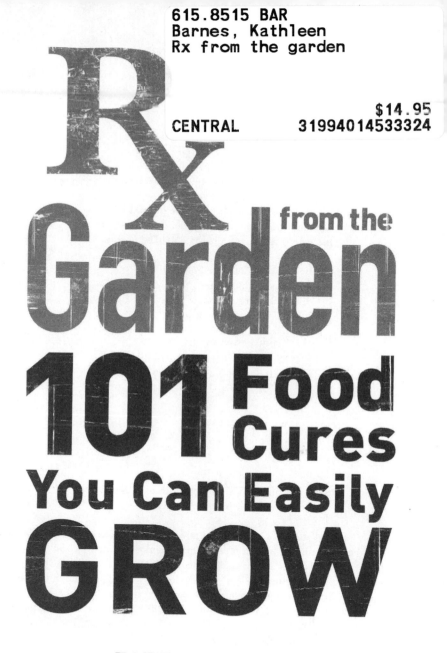

Rx from the Garden

101 Food Cures You Can Easily GROW

KATHLEEN BARNES

adamsmedia
Avon, Massachusetts

Published by
Adams Media, a division of F+W Media, Inc.
57 Littlefield Street, Avon, MA 02322. U.S.A.
www.adamsmedia.com

ISBN 10: 1-4405-1018-0
ISBN 13: 978-1-4405-1018-2
eISBN 10: 1-4405-1161-6
eISBN 13: 978-1-4405-1161-5

Printed in the United States of America.

10   9   8   7   6   5   4   3   2   1

Library of Congress Cataloging-in-Publication Data
is available from the publisher.

This book is intended as general information only, and should not be used to diagnose or treat any health condition. In light of the complex, individual, and specific nature of health problems, this book is not intended to replace professional medical advice. The ideas, procedures, and suggestions in this book are intended to supplement, not replace, the advice of a trained medical professional. Consult your physician before adopting any of the suggestions in this book, as well as about any condition that may require diagnosis or medical attention. The author and publisher disclaim any liability arising directly or indirectly from the use of this book

Many of the designations used by manufacturers and sellers to distinguish their product are claimed as trademarks. Where those designations appear in this book and Adams Media was aware of a trademark claim, the designations have been printed with initial capital letters.

This book is available at quantity discounts for bulk purchases.
For information, please call 1-800-289-0963.

Dedication

To Joe, for his infinite patience with the book birthing process and his endless love, support, and smoothies.

Acknowledgments

It takes a community to give birth to a book, and this one is no exception. *RX from the Garden* is not my work alone, but that of editors, designers, production folks, and marketers. I am most grateful to all of them, especially to my editor, Wendy Simard, whose patience and technological abilities far surpass mine.

Contents

PART 2: HOW TO GROW YOUR HEALING FOODS 113

Introduction

There is a certain romance to a garden. Whether it comes from a solitary basil plant on a window ledge, a potted tomato on an urban balcony, a small plot in a community garden, or a well-manicured full-scale spread, we humans take pride in growing our own food, feeding ourselves and relishing the flavor and vitality our homegrown foods bring to our bodies and spirits.

Most of us are aware that eating five or more servings of fruits and vegetables daily can prevent and even treat a host of diseases and illnesses. More and more of us are becoming aware of the importance of eating fresh wholesome local food that can keep us healthy and literally extend our lives. Many of us are trying to save money by growing our own food. Some of us even know the secrets of treating ailments and illnesses with herbs, fruits, and vegetables.

In this book, I hope to make those secrets common knowledge. I'm here to share with you the road to good health through the freshest of fruits and vegetables. I'll share with you what I've learned about health and healing with the right foods grown the right way. I'll share with you some of my successes, failures, and insights gained from a lifetime of gardening. I don't expect that you can or will grow every fruit and vegetable mentioned in this book. Most of us simply don't have the time or space. But I promise to offer you the secrets of healing with everyday foods available to everyone close to home. Back in the early '70s when I was just out of college, my friends and family thought I was a little wacky when I started talking about natural healing. They asked:

- Why brew a cup of sage tea when it was easier to take a swig of sugar-laden cough medicine?
- Why wrap an infected cut with chewed wood sorrel rather than slapping on a little triple antibiotic from a tube?
- Why chew a few fennel seeds or drink a cup of peppermint tea rather than take a Tums?

- Why compost my kitchen scraps when it is so easy to buy a bag of compost at the big-box garden center?
- Why slave away under a hot sun, watering and weeding and battling bugs and blights, when a juicy tomato was as close as my local supermarket?
- Why? Because all of these remedies and a simple lifestyle contribute to health and longevity. Even when I was in my twenties, healthy and longevity were my goals. Forty years later, they still are.

I've gardened all of my life. My earliest memories are of helping my grandmother weed her garden and gathering perfect roses wet with the morning dew. I've survived short growing seasons and harsh winters in northern New York state near the Canadian border. I've gardened in Asia and Africa, weathering the scorn of locals for my pitiful and often unsuccessful efforts.

Now I live in the mountains of western North Carolina and my gardens sprawl all over our one-acre lot. They're not always neat; in fact, they're not often neat. My compost bins are as far from scientific as you can get; nevertheless, I get "black gold" with the help of Mother Nature and Father Time. I have my share of garden failures, sometimes due to environmental conditions beyond my control, and more often due to my own shortcomings. And while I don't grow every morsel on our plates, in the summer I grow most of our vegetables and some of our fruit. I preserve a fair amount for winter soups, sauces, smoothies, and pies. I buy local whenever I can to reduce our pesticide load, support local growers, and prevent the pollution associated with huge semis trucking produce across the country to my local supermarket.

In return, my garden has rewarded me with delicious food, good health, exercise that I enjoy, and a golden farmer's tan. My aim in this book is to help you reap the same rewards. Because when it comes down to it, who could ask for more?

PART 1

FOOD AS HEALER

Let food be your medicine and medicine be your food.

—Hippocrates

CHAPTER 1

The Magic of Foods You Grow in Your Garden

There's nothing like biting into a juicy tomato, still warm from the summer sun. Many times, I am content to eat my entire meal right there in the garden. There are lots of reasons I can do this—snap off an asparagus stalk or eat a tomato without even washing it. I don't use pesticides or herbicides in my garden.

We live on a gravel road a mile from the nearest highway. The two cars that pass by daily don't worry me in terms of adding hydrocarbons to my crops, but it's certainly something to think about if you garden in a city or near a busy highway. We have a deep well so we are free of worry about additives to municipal water, and because we're at the top of a mountain very far from any agricultural enterprises, we're confident that our water quality is as good as it gets. In all, I think we avoid adding to our toxic load just about as well as is possible in modern society. We're not purists, but it's a pretty idyllic life, if you love mountains and fresh air and lots of space.

For many years, my husband and I lived in some of the world's biggest cities, but when the time came that, thanks to advancing technology, we could pursue our livelihoods almost anywhere, we high-tailed it to the Blue Ridge Mountains of western North Carolina. We've never looked back. Our lifestyle isn't for everyone, but I hope one or two of my thoughts here will inspire you to make even the smallest baby steps toward a more independent and healthy food supply.

In the spirit of full disclosure, there are two things you should know from the beginning:

1. I'm a lazy gardener, always looking for easier ways to keep things neat and orderly and improve my yield. As much as I love working in my garden, I don't want to spend *all* my time and energy there.
2. I'm a terrible cheapskate, always searching for ways to do things cheaper or, best of all, free.

If you're like-minded, please join me in my cheap and lazy ways. If you have a better work ethic, please write and inspire me: Kathleen@kathleenbarnes.com.

Growing vs. Buying Local

It's nearly impossible to grow everything you eat. But beyond what you're able to grow, one of the best things you can do for your health and the health of the planet is to buy produce (and meat) as locally as possible. There are three major reasons why:

1. Locally grown food is fresher than anything that has been trucked in and therefore has more nutrients. Most foods begin to lose their nutrients the moment they are picked, so a tomato that grew in your backyard or in a garden three miles from you will have much more vitamin C, lycopene, beta carotene, and on and on.

   The veggies I don't grow come mostly from Crystal, who has a little ad hoc stand at the bottom of our road. They're not officially organic, since organic certification is a long and complicated process, but she doesn't use pesticides or herbicides and she picks many of her wares fresh in the mornings and brings them out to sell. It doesn't get much more local than that. Many local producers follow the same way of thinking.

You probably have a farmer's market in your town—even the smallest burgs and the biggest cities have them. Patronize your local farmers for your own health and to help boost your local economy.

2. The environmental cost of locally produced food is lower because we're not using gas to transport the food long distances. There's a concept called "food miles," which translates to "how much does your food really cost the environment when your lettuce is being trucked in from California to North Carolina?" Of course, what immediately follows is that a $2 plastic carton of California strawberries—available year round, by the way—might have contributed to putting a ton of carbon dioxide into the atmosphere as it was trucked across the country.

    A peripheral argument for buying local: less packaging. You're not going to find those environmentally costly plastic clamshells or Styrofoam trays at the farmers' market, and more often than not, you won't even find a plastic grocery bag there, since most of us have by now been trained to bring our own shopping bags.

3. Local is almost always cheaper. When the supermarket is charging $2 a pound for California tomatoes early in our season, you can usually buy them for half that from local produce sellers who may be trucking them from 100 or fewer miles away! As summer progresses, a dozen ears of local corn can cost a mere $2, making it hardly worth the effort to grow your own and try to fight off the raccoons and other pests that are just as eagerly awaiting the exact moment of ripeness.

The obvious question that follows the "buy local" soapbox speech is "What happens when winter comes?"

Good question. If you can't grow oranges where you live, that doesn't mean you shouldn't eat them—they are one of the most healthy foods available. So buy them in the winter. We can't grow ginger here, so I buy it freely and happily, knowing it has a host of benefits for our health and knowing it cost the environment to bring it here.

If you live in a colder zone, you can grow lettuce in a cold frame during the winter and it usually survives to give you fresh greens in the winter months. Plus, you can always rely on dehydrated and frozen goodies to help you make it through the winter.

There is a delightful story of a family who decided to eat only what could be produced within 100 miles of their home for an entire year. It was a great concept, but in reality, it was extremely difficult because they lived in British Columbia and some things were simply not available, especially in winter. Among the shortfalls: no source of oil for cooking or dressings. Oil is an essential component of our nutrition, and without it we cannot survive. The wise family of locavores decided an exception had to be made for cooking oil.

We are no longer a society of hunters and gatherers. If we were, we would know enough to put away seeds and nuts and rose hips and dried, pickled, salted, and fermented foods to get us through the winter, not only to keep our bellies full, but to provide the nutrients we so desperately need.

Is Organic Better?

This is an issue that has captivated the imaginations of many for a number of years. Organic foods are invariably more expensive than nonorganic. Crop yields are smaller without all the chemicals, but whatever the reason and however great your commitment to support organic farmers, it's hard to stomach paying $5 for a tomato in January.

There have been research findings that indicate organic foods are more nutritious than conventionally grown foods. That certainly makes sense to me, but sometimes it is simply too much for the budget.

However, there are certain foods for which you should make the greatest effort to buy organic. These foods are dubbed the Dirty Dozen, the common foods that carry the heaviest chemical load. Frequently they are foods that we eat unpeeled, which in some cases increases the potential toxin load. For example, since you're not going to eat the thick peel, buying organic oranges is less important than buying organic peaches or strawberries, where so much goodness is in the peel.

BUY ORGANIC: THE DIRTY DOZEN
- Peaches (highest pesticide load)
- Apples
- Bell peppers
- Celery
- Nectarines
- Strawberries
- Cherries
- Kale
- Lettuce
- Grapes
- Carrots
- Pears

Also, if you're a coffee drinker, consider buying organic since coffee beans are among the most pesticide-laden crops in the world, right up there along with cotton. (But that's a subject for another book. . . .)

Aren't Supplements Just as Good?

It's true, our soils have been depleted of many of their nutrients, and commercially produced fruits and vegetables may not be as wealthy in vitamins and minerals as they once were. But if you're growing your own food and know what is going into the soil, there's no reason to believe your veggies aren't giving you optimal nutrition. I know that many people wonder, wouldn't it just be easier to pop a few pills and get our nutrients from supplements?

It might be easier, but it might not give you the nutrients you think it would.

Foods are extremely complex amalgamations of nutrients. Consider the lowly onion. Actually, it deserves a whole lot of respect, as it's one of the most healing foods we know!

Here's what's in the onion you just chopped into your salad:

- **Quercetin:** antihistamine and anti-inflammatory
- **Allicin:** antimicrobial (fights bacterial, viral and fungal infections)
- **Sulforaphane:** fights cancer, diabetes and microbial infections
- **Chromium:** key to the proper metabolism of sugars and fats; essential to opotimal brain function
- **Vitamin C:** boosts immune system function, improves wound healing, strengthens collagen and connective tissue, helps remove cancer-causing nitrosamines from the body, and much more
- **Fiber:** ushers excess fats from the digestive tract, prevents constipation and hemorrhoids, assists in weight control, helps prevent heart disease, cancer, diabetes, diverticular disease, gallstones, and kidney stones
- **Manganese:** aids in the formation of bones, connective tissue, blood-clotting factors, and sex hormones; plays a role in calcium absorption, blood sugar metabolism, and fat and carbohydrate metabolism
- **Vitamin B6:** contributes to the manufacture of the calming brain chemical serotonin, improves immune system function, breaks down carbohydrates, regulates estrogen and progesterone, reduces risk of heart disease
- **Tryptophan:** natural antidepressant, lowers blood pressure, reduces hyperactivity in children, relieves restless leg syndrome
- **Folate:** prevents birth defects, formation of red and white blood cells, maintains and repairs cell, removes homocysteine from blood, lowering risk of heart disease
- **Potassium:** reduces blood pressure; lowers risk of heart attack and stroke; relieves anxiety, irritability and stress; relieves fatigue
- **Copper:** promotes proper growth, essential for energy production, red blood cell formation, reduction of cholesterol, important in bone growth, helps regulate heart rhythm, contributes to wound healing connective tissue, eye and hair health

All this and just 60 calories. No fat. Great taste. How does that stack up to a pill? I never heard of an onion pill, but eating an onion is a lot like taking a multivitamin.

My point is this: No food is made up of just one nutrient. Not only do we need *all* of these nutrients, scientists are slowly beginning to realize what moms and grandmothers have known since the beginning of time: The whole is greater than the sum of the parts. There is a synergy between these nutrients that makes each one more powerful and enhances all the others.

So get your nutrients from food as much as you can. Don't hesitate to take a multivitamin—you never know if your soil is low on selenium or boron—but look to a healthy diet for most of your nutrients. Conversely, don't think you can eat junk food all day long and make up for it by popping a few strategic supplements. It just doesn't work that way.

For the Love of the Garden

The health benefits of spending time in the garden go far beyond the nutritive value of the foods you grow. Gardening is a wonderful form of exercise. Exercise physiologists say it is at least as effective in calorie burning as jogging, but in my humble opinion, it's much more fun!

You'll feel the burn as you lift baskets of compost, till the soil, carry water, and pull weeds.

Exposure to fresh air and the elements also make gardening an effective stress reliever. Since I work from home, I'm lucky I can take gardening breaks throughout the day. Spending just ten minutes pulling weeds or pruning an overgrown oregano plant allows my mind to rest and the stress to simply flow into the earth, leaving me refreshed and ready to return to the task at hand with renewed enthusiasm and focus.

Whether reducing stress is your goal, or keeping your weight in an optimal range, inside this book you'll find everything you need to know and grow to help you stay on track, healthy and happy. Treating your garden as your doctor can make your life full. I know that's how I feel.

CHAPTER 2

101 Ailments You Can Prevent and Treat with Food

Most of us don't think of the food on plates quite literally as medicine, but when you're finished reading this chapter, you'll know you can treat and prevent a wide range of ailments simply with powerful healing properties of the fruits of your garden labor.

ACNE

YOUR GARDEN RX: dried beans, berries, watermelon, walnuts

When you were as teenager, your mom probably told you that chocolate and those yummy greasy French fries caused acne, but for once, she was wrong. Hormone fluctuation is the major cause of acne, which is why it rears its ugly head at puberty, often during the menstrual cycle in a woman's childbearing years, and again at menopause if you're a woman or andropause if you're a man. Stress is also a factor, as can be those harsh products you use in a vain attempt to make the zits go away.

Conventional medicine often treats acne with long courses of antibiotics, a risky plan because it can reduce your body's ability to respond to antibiotics when you really need them—to treat a serious infection, for example. Your best defense is healthy, clean, hydrated skin. And, of course, a few healers from the garden.

YOUR GARDEN TO THE RESCUE

Beans are a good source of B vitamins and zinc that nourish your skin and keep it healthy. **Berries**, especially blueberries, raspberries, and cranberries, are rich in phytochemicals that help protect skin cells.

Watermelon rind (that's right) rubbed on your skin may help move the lymph through your skin and keep those zits from erupting. It also exfoliates your skin and adds healthy vitamins A, B, and C, which are absorbed right through your skin.

Walnuts are rich in healthy omega-3 fatty acids, oils that help keep your skin cells plump and flexible.

ADRENAL FATIGUE

YOUR GARDEN RX: sunflower seeds, parsley, beets and beet greens, broccoli
The adrenals are two tiny glands that sit on top of the kidneys and play a vital role in the manufacture of more than fifty hormones, including the stress hormone cortisol.

When your body loses its ability to respond appropriately to stress, adrenal fatigue sets in. People with adrenal fatigue or a more serious condition called adrenal exhaustion (also called Addison's disease) feel tired, weak, and cold.

Some key signs and symptoms of adrenal fatigue include salt cravings, increased blood sugar under stress, increased PMS, perimenopausal or menopausal symptoms, low blood pressure, mild depression, lack of energy, decreased ability to handle stress, muscle weakness, absentmindedness, decreased sex drive, mild constipation alternating with diarrhea, as well as many others.

The most effective treatment for adrenal fatigue is stress management. Conventional medicine treats adrenal fatigue with a variety of hormone and glandular extracts and, in extreme cases, with hydrocortisone, a steroid that can actually make the adrenals weaker rather than stronger.

YOUR GARDEN TO THE RESCUE
Sunflower seeds are a great source of the B vitamins that are depleted when we are overstressed.

Parsley is mineral-rich, so it helps restore the natural store of minerals depleted during adrenal fatigue. It is high in vitamin C (300 mg per cup), which promotes the production of stress-reducing hormones.

Beets and beet greens are high in organic sodium, so they can help bring low sodium levels back to normal in order to improve adrenal function.

Broccoli has, among many other nutrients, high levels of pantothenic acid, which promotes the production of calming hormones to neutralize the stress hormones.

RX from Outside Your Garden

Wild yam promotes the natural production of progesterone, another adrenal function that falters with adrenal fatigue.

ALCOHOLISM (ALSO SEE DEPRESSION)

YOUR GARDEN RX: spinach and dark green leafy vegetables, cabbage, asparagus, dried beans

Alcoholism is a terrible disease that can cause malnutrition and brain and liver damage as well as emotional turmoil. Primary among the effects of alcoholism is severe thiamine deficiency marked by wasting, appetite loss, nausea, and other digestive troubles as well as loss of muscle mass, nerve disorders, and depression.

Since few people recognize they are on their way to alcoholism until they are already in trouble, treatment is more often needed than prevention. During the time of withdrawal from alcohol, it's a good idea to eliminate simple carbohydrates as much as possible, since these sugars are similar to the alcohol sugar and may trigger alcohol cravings.

Most of us know someone who is an alcoholic and we know the toll it can take on families. Treatment is difficult and is of uncertain effectiveness.

YOUR GARDEN TO THE RESCUE

Spinach and other **dark green leafy vegetables** and **asparagus** are good sources of folates, a group of B vitamins that are often depleted when someone is alcohol dependant. These foods, eaten freely, can help restore nutritional health.

Cabbage and other brassicas or cruciferous vegetables like broccoli, cauliflower, and bok choy help detoxify the system and act as a diuretic to flush out toxins. Cabbage is also an excellent liver tonic, so it may help the liver recover its function.

Dried beans have a high fiber content that will help stabilize blood sugars and reduce alcohol cravings.

RX from Outside Your Garden

Kudzu. Unless you're a Southerner, you may not be familiar with The Vine That Ate the South, but this Asian native is well known for its ability to reduce alcohol intake. Although you wouldn't grow it in your garden, since it is incredibly invasive, kudzu root can be very useful in treating alcoholism. You won't have to dig beside the highway; it's available as a supplement.

ALLERGIES

YOUR GARDEN RX: garlic, onions, apples, chamomile

Allergies are your body's response to what it perceives as an invader. With allergies, your immune system reacts or overreacts to a stimulus—whether it's triggered by a particular food (eggs and peanuts are common food allergens), penicillin, pollen, dust, bee stings, mold, pet dander, or latex or some similar substance—even though in reality that stimulus may not be at all threatening to you.

When this happens, your body releases histamine, a chemical that can cause a wide variety of symptoms ranging from hives and frantic itching to sneezing, sinus congestion, swelling, and, in serious cases of food and drug allergies, lowered blood pressure, unconsciousness, and even death.

YOUR GARDEN TO THE RESCUE

Garlic and **onions** save the day! Add **apples** in the same category because all three of these common garden foods contain a flavonoid called quercetin, which controls the release of histamines during an allergic reaction. Quercetin also reduces the production of leukotrienes, compounds that cause even more severe inflammation than do histamines.

Chamomile is a daisylike herb whose flowers make a calming and soothing tea. In addition, chamomile is a source of natural antihistamines and quercetin. It may also be helpful in an anaphylactic (severe allergic reaction) episode, but it shouldn't ever take the place of a visit to the emergency room if you know you are severely allergic to peanuts, bee stings, or other allergens and have been exposed to them. Drinking a cup or two of chamomile tea daily can help suppress the histaminic reaction, and over time, may make your allergic reactions less irritating or even help them disappear.

ALZHEIMER'S DISEASE, MEMORY LOSS, AND DEMENTIA

YOUR GARDEN RX: black-eyed peas, lentils, avacados, red grapes, blueberries, sunflower seeds, spinach, asparagus, celery, sage
As we age, many of us become a "little forgetful" and for some, the problem is much worse than a little forgetfulness from time to time.

Alzheimer's disease is the most common cause of dementia, and a diagnosis is a terrible blow both to the patient and family. However, there are many foods and herbs that can help.

YOUR GARDEN TO THE RESCUE

Black-eyed peas are a good source of B vitamins, especially folic acid, B12, and B6, and those B vitamins are excellent ways of reducing high levels of an amino acid called homocysteine that is linked to heart attacks and strokes. Research also shows us that as we age, our B12 levels drop, and memory loss is one of the earliest symptoms of B12 deficiency. So it makes sense to load up on foods rich in B vitamins, including **lentils, avocados, sunflower seeds, spinach**, and **asparagus**.

Red grapes and their powerhouse antioxidant *resveratrol* help keep free radicals from building up the biological equivalent of rust in our systems, including in our brains. In addition to resveratrol, grapes are good sources of a number of nutrients that help thin your blood, reduce cell inflammation, and protect your brain cells.

Blueberries are the king of antioxidants, and studies show that blueberries can help improve mental performance.

Celery is a rich source of luteolin, a compound that research says may help lower levels of the proteins that create plaque in the brain characteristic of people with Alzheimer's.

Sage has been shown to improve memory, even in young people taking tests as well as in patients with Alzheimer's. Scientists think sage may help acetylcholine production to improve nerve communication that is often lacking in people with various types of dementia.

RX from Outside Your Garden

I can't close this section without mentioning turmeric, the curry spice that I'm sure you won't be growing in your garden but that has so many health benefits it is considered a superfood. People in India, where turmeric is used in daily cooking, rarely suffer from Alzheimer's. Scientists believe it can prevent the buildup of Alzheimer's-related plaque in the brain.

ANEMIA

YOUR GARDEN RX: potatoes, dried beans, pumpkin, arugula, spinach
The most common type of anemia is caused by low iron levels in the blood, but there are other more complicated types. For our purposes here, we'll be talking about iron deficiency anemia that occurs when your red blood cells aren't carrying enough life-giving oxygen.

If you've been diagnosed with iron deficiency anemia, you are not getting enough iron in your diet or you are losing blood, perhaps through heavy menstrual periods. You're probably thinking about seafood and red meats as the best sources of iron, but you may be surprised to learn that many foods from your garden are also iron-rich.

In general, adults need about 15 mg of iron a day. It requires special attention to get enough from vegetable sources in an absorbable form, but you can do it. If you're a vegetarian and getting your iron solely from vegetable sources (which include dried beans), you'll find that you'll improve the absorbability of iron by including foods with vitamin C in the same meal.

YOUR GARDEN TO THE RESCUE

Potatoes are a good combo vegetable, containing a modest amount of iron (2.8 mg) with vitamin C (20 mg). **Pumpkin** is also a good source of iron, with 1.7 mg per half-cup serving, and pumpkin seeds are even better with 4.3 mg per one-ounce serving. **Dried beans** and lentils are also good sources of iron.

Spinach and **arugula** and dark green leafy vegetables are good sources of iron (for those of a certain generation, think of Popeye and his energy-giving can of spinach), minerals, and vitamin C.

RX from Outside Your Garden

If you're a beekeeper, your own honey may also be helpful. Because your allergic reactions may be caused by local pollens, the honey that results from bees collecting those pollens may act as the antidote to the perceived immune system threat caused by the allergens. If you don't keep bees, try to find honey made from local pollens not more than a few miles from your home.

ANXIETY

YOUR GARDEN RX: lettuce, peaches, raspberries, blueberries, borage, lavender, basil

All of us have experienced anxiety at one time or another. For some of us, it can be debilitating as we scroll through seemingly endless past grievances and possibilities of disaster in the future.

Anxiety can have deep effects on the rest of your system if it keeps your body too long in the fight-or-flight response (see Adrenal Fatigue). It often is also the flip side of depression. Severe anxiety is also sometimes called anxiety disorder, posttraumatic stress syndrome, or panic disorder. It interferes with sleep and causes high blood pressure and irritability. Calming foods and herbs will help in the short and long term.

YOUR GARDEN TO THE RESCUE

Lettuce has traditionally been used as a calmative, often in juice form. It is considered a natural tranquilizer and also calms stress-related headaches.

Peaches are soothing to the entire nervous system and are helpful for a host of stress-related problems, including digestive issues, skin irritation, and heartburn. They may promote healthy sleep.

Nerve-soothing vitamin C and other beneficial nutrients that counteract the excess cortisol released during an anxiety attack are plentiful in **raspberries** and **blueberries**. Teas made from the leaves of these plants are also very soothing.

Basil is an age-old calmative that has been used to reduce anxiety, lift spirits, and improve concentration. Holy basil, a different variety of the familiar herb usually grown in India, is also good for soothing anxiety.

APPETITE CONTROL

YOUR GARDEN RX: apples, potatoes, grapes, cabbage, leafy greens like boy choy and arugula
Trying to rein in an overenthusiastic appetite is extremely difficult. Sometimes stress triggers overeating and sometimes there are lapses in brain chemistry that fail to register when you are full.

Vegetables and fruits high in fiber will really help dial down your hunger and stay with you long enough for you to feel satisfied for hours.

YOUR GARDEN TO THE RESCUE

Not only are **apples** high in fiber, they also contain nutrients that help you feel full quickly and then turn off food cravings for hours.

Potatoes (baked, please, and with a *small* amount of butter or sour cream, since fats help trigger those fullness hormones) are another great source of fiber, as is **cabbage**.

Grapes have a high sugar content, but just a few will help bring your appetite under control, precisely because of their intense sweetness.

Salad greens like **bok choy, arugula, mesclun**, and **endive** stimulate your taste buds, helping you feel satisfied while the fiber actually helps slow the flow of glucose into your bloodstream, keeping blood sugars steady and controlling sugar swings that trigger cravings.

APPETITE LOSS

YOUR GARDEN RX: tomatoes, peaches, apricots, red currants, dill, caraway

Loss of appetite is a symptom of a variety of illnesses, but the most common cause in today's high-pressured society is stress. While some people eat more when they are stressed, others eat less or lose their appetites entirely.

People who are ill or are recovering from an illness often experience loss of appetite, as do frail elderly people.

Lifestyle choices that cause appetite loss include heavy alcohol consumption, smoking, and heavy sugar consumption, especially in soft drinks. Low vitamin C levels can cause loss of appetite, so eating foods rich in vitamin C may help.

Small, frequent meals may encourage greater food intake.

YOUR GARDEN TO THE RESCUE

Tomatoes and other garden foods high in vitamin C, such as **green peppers**, are often used to stimulate appetite.

Dill has natural calming properties, so adding dill to your foods can help relax you and relieve stress. In addition, its strong flavor can help make food more appetizing.

Caraway, those pungent seeds often found in rye bread, helps stimulate appetite by increasing the flow of digestive juices and encourages a better appetite. Chew a few seeds before eating for an appetite stimulant.

Some sources say that tangy fruits like **peaches, apricots**, and **red currants** will also stimulate appetite.

ARTHRITIS

Arthritis is divided into osteoarthritis, an inflammatory condition, and rheumatoid arthritis, an autoimmune disease, These two most common types of the disease have very different causes.

OSTEOARTHRITIS

YOUR GARDEN RX: hot peppers, cantaloupe, broccoli, strawberries, bell peppers, grapes

Often called "wear and tear" arthritis, this type of joint pain results from the deterioration of the cartilage, which acts as a cushion in the joints. This can be the result of aging—ironically, it's more prevalent among those who have been very active as runners, tennis players, or athletes of almost any type—and it can also be caused by injury and the gravitational effects of obesity. Osteoarthritis affects as many as 10 percent of Americans. It most commonly occurs in the hips and knees, although it can also be a problem in the neck, spine, elbows, wrists, hands, ankles, and feet—virtually any major joint. The deterioration of cushioning between joints leads to stiffness, pain, and inflammation. The pain and inflammation cycle can be controlled naturally without the dangerous prescription and over-the-counter drugs, which can have serious side effects. Some foods may actually help rebuild damaged cartilage.

YOUR GARDEN TO THE RESCUE

Hot peppers can offer fast pain relief because they are loaded with salicylates, which are anti-inflammatories that act like aspirin, and capsaicin, the actual "heat" of the peppers, which blocks the chemical in nerves that transmits pain. You can get the same effect from eating hot sauces made from peppers and cayenne pepper. Topical poultices made from hot peppers can also be helpful, if you can take the heat!

Vitamin C–rich foods like **cantaloupe, broccoli, strawberries, grapes**, and **bell peppers** can also help keep the remaining cartilage strong by reducing inflammation and enhancing production of collagen, which strengthens soft tissue.

Red grapes are an excellent source of resveratrol, quercetin, and saponins, all highly effective anti-inflammatories.

RX from Outside Your Garden

Ginger and turmeric are powerful anti-inflammatories that you're unlikely to grow in your garden but will be helpful in relieving the pain caused by inflammation.

RHEUMATOID ARTHRITIS

YOUR GARDEN RX: **green grapes, green beans, celery, cucumbers, lettuce, butternut squash, peas, dried beans**

This form of arthritis is an autoimmune disease, which means that the body's defense system attacks its own cartilage as though it is a foreign invader. Rheumatoid arthritis (RA) can be crippling, and it is immensely painful. The symptoms of both kinds of arthritis are similar, and the treatments for osteoarthritis sufferers will also be of benefit to those with the immune type. In addition, there is some evidence that rheumatoid arthritis may be aggravated by certain foods. Many people with the disease have been able to determine which foods are their individual "triggers" and eliminate them from their diets. Most commonly, these trigger foods are milk products and gluten.

YOUR GARDEN TO THE RESCUE

Green grapes, green beans, celery, cucumbers, lettuce, and **butternut squash** are excellent sources of a pigment called beta-cryptoxanthin, a carotenoid found in brightly colored fruits and vegetables that lowers the risk of rheumatoid arthritis.

In general, it's a good idea to increase your intake of **all types of fruit** if you have been diagnosed with RA, even to the point of drinking an 8-ounce glass of juice a day.

The zinc found in all kinds of **peas** and **dried beans** may also help restore immune system health, bringing an overactive immune system back into balance.

RX from Outside Your Garden

Going a little afield here, I'm guessing that most of my readers aren't fish farmers or olive grove owners, so you won't literally be growing these foods in your garden, but among the most effective treatments for both major types of arthritis is the regular consumption of inflammation-fighting foods like olive oil and salmon and tuna.

ASTHMA

YOUR GARDEN RX: **strawberries, broccoli, tomatoes, citrus fruits, onions, garlic, horseradish, spinach, borage, dill**

Acute asthma attacks can be life-threatening, so please don't stop the prescription medications your doctor has given you. However, over time you may find your need for inhalers will diminish with the help of foods from your garden. Asthma causes inflammation of the airways (bronchial tubes) making it hard to breathe and causing chronic cough, wheezing, and shortness of breath. It can also cause a buildup of mucus in the bronchial tubes, making it harder and harder to breathe. The onset of a full-blown attack when the bronchial tubes spasm can be truly frightening and, without emergency care, can be fatal.

YOUR GARDEN TO THE RESCUE

Vitamin C is a natural antihistamine, meaning it stops the extreme inflammatory response that triggers the wheezing and runny nose, so eating all foods high in vitamin C will be helpful, including **strawberries, broccoli, tomatoes**, and **citrus fruits**, if you're lucky enough to live in a place where you can grow them. Some research also suggests that eating lots of vitamin C–rich foods can reduce the severity of asthma attacks. Note: If you're eating citrus fruits, try squeezing the peels and inhaling the aroma. A substance called limonene, which is found in the citrus peel, helps soothe the airways. You can also eat the peels, but wash them well to sure to remove any contaminants that might be present.

Onions and **garlic** are rich sources of two major anti-inflammatory and anti-asthmatic compounds, quercetin and cepaene, that can help soothe irritated airways.

If you've ever taken a big breath of **horseradish, wasabi, cayenne**, or other spicy foods, you've probably noticed that your airways immediately open up if you've been experiencing any stuffiness. This holds true for asthma as well. I don't recommend regularly inhaling the fumes of these pungent foods, but adding them to salads, or better yet to hot soups and stews, will have the same effect.

Leafy greens like **spinach** are good sources of vitamin E, which helps your body release soothing compounds to relax muscles in the lungs.

Borage is a natural decongestant and expectorant, so it can help reduce the mucus in the airways, and **dill** is a traditional relaxant of the bronchial system.

BACK PAIN

YOUR GARDEN RX: chili peppers, cherries, red grapes, mint

Back pain is the most common pain complaint among Americans, with about 25 percent of us saying it regularly affects our work, sleep, and ability to function in normal daily activities. Back pain can have a wide range of causes including injury, muscle spasm, deterioration of joints, and nerve entrapment.

Conventional medicine treats back pain either by ignoring it or by prescribing painkillers, muscle relaxants, and even antidepressants. Steroid shots are common, and, thankfully, most doctors consider back surgery to be the last resort. All of these treatments carry with them side effects and danger, and their effectiveness is variable.

YOUR GARDEN TO THE RESCUE

Chili peppers are the source of capsaicin, a powerful painkiller that is relatively unique in the plant world because it provides quick relief. In many ways, it works like aspirin without the potentially harmful side effects and it temporarily blocks a compound called "substance P" that transmits pain signals along the nerves to the brain. Hot peppers are best used topically for back pain. You can easily make a salve containing chopped peppers, although eating them and spiking your food with hot sauces made from peppers will also help.

If you make a salve, you'll find that it will burn when you first rub it on your skin. This is perfectly normal, but may be a little unsettling until you adapt to it. Wash your hands carefully afterward to avoid inadvertently rubbing it into your eyes (or somewhere worse).

If your back pain is caused by sports-related muscle injury or spasm, eating tart **cherries** may be preventive because they contain substances that can help protect the *quadratus lumborum*, the muscle most often implicated in lower back pain.

A diet that includes **red grapes** (including moderate consumption of red wine) can be an avenue to pain relief thanks to the anti-inflammatory action of resveratrol, quercetin, and saponins.

Also, I urge you to find a good yoga teacher. Be sure to tell your teacher about your back pain. Yoga can be one of the most effective back pain remedies.

BAD BREATH

YOUR GARDEN RX: celery, sage, parsley, fennel

Bad breath isn't a disease, but it certainly can be uncomfortable for you and your loved ones. It is often the result of poor oral hygiene and is usually an indicator of gum disease.

Bad breath may also be a symptom of some more serious underlying problem such as kidney failure, liver disease, or diabetes. People with chronic respiratory problems often have bad breath because of dry mouth.

We all know that eating certain sulfurous foods like our beloved onions and garlic can also cause temporary bad breath, as can the consumption of alcoholic beverages and dairy foods, especially cheese.

If you improve your oral hygiene and that doesn't relieve your bad breath, see your doctor to find out if there is an underlying cause.

YOUR GARDEN TO THE RESCUE

Celery can work like a natural toothbrush since it is so fibrous, so if your bad breath is due to poor oral hygiene, it can help clean that gummy food residue off your teeth. It is an excellent addition to your lunch bag.

Many natural toothpastes contain **sage**, for good reason since it is a good source of menthol, thymol and 1,8-cineole, all known to help sweeten breath.

Chewing on a sprig of **parsley** after a meal can immediately neutralize offensive odors because it is one of the richest sources of chlorophyll, a natural deodorizer. If you're a fan of Indian food like I am, you'll notice that there is often a bowl of **fennel** seeds next to the door to help freshen your breath and to encourage digestion after a meal.

BLADDER INFECTIONS

YOUR GARDEN RX: celery, blueberries, turnips, cranberries, mint, thyme, other herbs

Bladder infection is largely a women's problem, affecting 20 percent of us at some time in our lives, and most often sexually active women during their childbearing years. If you've ever experienced the burning, constant pressure to urinate, abdominal pain, and fever of a bladder infection, you know how unpleasant it can be. Men can experience bladder infections, as well, especially if they have prostate dysfunction.

Conventional medicine usually treats bladder infections, also called urinary cystitis or urinary tract infections, with antibiotics. While you shouldn't let the misery go on for weeks at a time, these natural remedies may give you relief in a matter of days.

YOUR GARDEN TO THE RESCUE

Dried herbs that contain the substances cineole or thymol are perhaps the most potent healers of the bladder because they have antiseptic properties that are specific to it. Fortunately, you can grow most of them in your own garden and they make a delicious tea. Among the best in these categories are all types of **mints, rosemary, fennel, tarragon, basil, thyme**, and **oregano**. When you first start to feel that urinary urgency or the faintest burning, a tea containing any or all of these herbs can stop an infection before it takes hold.

Celery is a good source of relief from pain and inflammation as well as a diuretic that relieves fluid buildup.

Cranberries are probably the best-known natural remedy for bladder infection, although most of us probably can't grow them in our gardens. **Blueberries** are a great alternative, with many of the same healing properties of cranberries, including some antibacterial effects.

Turnips are a good source of sulfur compounds that have been historically valued for their urinary health benefits, including helping to relieve fluid buildup and even helping break up kidney stones.

BLOOD SUGAR—HIGH/LOW (ALSO SEE DIABETES)

YOUR GARDEN RX: beans and legumes, sweet potatoes, cabbage, potatoes, walnuts

Low blood sugar (hypoglycemia) indicates that your body is lacking glucose—its basic fuel source. You can experience hypoglycemia if you haven't eaten for twelve hours or more, of if you have a glucose/insulin imbalance or, more likely, if your pancreas's production of glucose-balancing insulin is too high to balance the glucose in your blood. The occasional bout of hypoglycemia usually isn't serious, but repeated episodes can indicate diabetes. Symptoms may be similar to drunkenness, making hypoglycemia especially serious if you are driving.

High blood sugar (hyperglycemia) is an excess of glucose in your bloodstream. While it may be seem the opposite of hypoglycemia, the two conditions usually go hand-in-hand and are often precursors of diabetes. Hyperglycemia could be the result of eating too much sugary food, but more likely it indicates that insulin production or absorption is inadequate to balance your sugar intake. Most people with high blood sugar are unaware of it because the symptoms are subtle, but those symptoms can include excessive hunger, thirst, and frequent urination.

It is not unusual for sugar levels to swing between high and low and for sugar cravings to result from low blood sugar.

It's best to eat complex carbohydrates like whole grains and proteins when your sugar is low and to generally center your diet on foods low on the glycemic index, a measure of the effects of carbohydrates on blood sugar levels, to keep your sugars steady and help you avoid a sugar-swing roller coaster.

RX from Outside Your Garden

Several studies show that cinnamon can help balance blood sugar, so adding a teaspoon a day to your morning cereal or stirring it into your tea can be very helpful.

Because fruit is particularly high in sugar, it is best to avoid high fruit consumption and certainly to avoid juices—which are concentrated fruit sugar and can cause blood sugar swings.

YOUR GARDEN TO THE RESCUE
Potatoes, sweet potatoes, all types of dried beans and **legumes, cabbage,** and **nuts** are excellent sources of fiber that digest slowly and release their natural sugars into your bloodstream slowly and steadily. They also give you a balancing protein boost.

BODY ODOR

YOUR GARDEN RX: spinach, chamomile, parsley, cilantro, mint
Sweat is the body's natural cooling system. If you didn't sweat, you'd overheat, dehydrate, and you could even die of heat stroke. With sweat can come body odor, so for social reasons most of us use commercial deodorants.

Of course, we sweat when we're exposed to warm temperatures or when we exercise, but anxiety and emotional stress can also cause sweating.

Offensive odors are usually caused by bacterial growth in sweat, so frequent bathing with soap and water is all that is needed in most cases. If you are a heavy consumer of onions and garlic, be aware that those foods may actually cause a body odor beyond bad breath, and if you're a heavy drinker, the alcohol can become an offensive part of your sweat.

If possible, avoid commercial antiperspirants that have aluminum chlorhydrate as a principal ingredient. Aluminum has been implicated as an underlying case in many conditions, including Alzheimer's disease.

YOUR GARDEN TO THE RESCUE
Chlorophyll helps cleanse you from the inside out, literally binding with toxins and ushering them out of your body. **Parsley, cilantro,** and **mints** are all good sources of chlorophyll, so eating them (especially fresh) can give you natural deodorant protection.

Chamomile tea is calming and relaxing, so it can stop nerves that trigger anxiety-related sweating. Some people even use chamomile teabags in the bath or wipe their underarms with them to curb body odor.

Spinach, cucumbers, and other foods high in zinc may help restore natural zinc levels if they have become too low, causing, among other things, offensive body odors.

BONE LOSS

YOUR GARDEN RX: beans, kale, broccoli, carrots, spinach, potatoes
Bone health is a vital concern for almost everyone as we age, particularly for postmenopausal women. Low bone mass, also called osteopenia, affects 34 million Americans, although many may be unaware of their condition. When low bone mass reaches a critical level, it is called osteoporosis, a serious weakening of the bones that results in bone deterioration and fractures.

With a good diet and exercise program, your goal will be to reverse the loss of bone mass.

As we age, bones lose their minerals and become structurally weaker than when we were young. Abundant research shows that the more active you are as a young person, the greater your bone density and the lower your risk of bone loss as you age. Weight-bearing exercise (walking, jogging, tennis, and so on) is important for everyone, but it is essential to preserve bone strength as you age.

Since bones are composed of a variety of minerals, a mineral-rich diet will help keep them strong, as will optimal intakes of vitamins D and K, which enhance absorption of the minerals by the bones.

YOUR GARDEN TO THE RESCUE

Calcium-rich foods are part of the equation, but you'll need to balance calcium with other trace minerals to avoid calcium overload, which won't help your bones at all. **Broccoli** and **kale** are good sources of calcium and they're an excellent source of other essential minerals, like potassium, selenium, and the vitamins that help absorb them, including vitamin K.

All **dried beans**—especially dark-colored beans like black beans and dark red kidney beans—are a good source of protein, which helps keep bones strong. In addition, the protein helps your body form collagen to help hold the minerals in bones.

Vitamin A, like the rich stores found in **carrots** and **spinach**, are important elements of remodeling bones. Too much retinol—an element of vitamin A found in cheese and eggs—can contribute to bone loss, but the healthy carotenoids in **carrots** and **spinach** are the "good guys."

Potatoes are an excellent of potassium that help alkalize your body, balancing the bone-softening effects of an acidic diet characterized by a diet high in red meat.

RX from Outside Your Garden

Unrefined sea salt contains dozens of trace minerals, many of which are needed for bone strength. To get the best, look for a telltale pinkish color that lets you know all the minerals are intact.

BRONCHITIS

YOUR GARDEN RX: onions and garlic, elderberries, hot peppers, thyme, turnips, kohlrabi, mustard greens, horseradish

Bronchitis is an inflammation of the main airways to the lungs that often follows a cold or flu. It may be short-lived or it can become a chronic condition. A cough the produces phlegm and produces wheezing, a sore throat, and perhaps even difficulty breathing, chest pain, and nasal congestion could be bronchitis.

Children and smokers are very susceptible to bronchitis.

Conventional medicine treats bronchitis with antibiotics, but growing evidence shows that although the condition is inflammatory, it is still likely that it's not bacterial but instead caused by viruses and fungi, against which antibiotics are ineffective.

YOUR GARDEN TO THE RESCUE

If you're looking for an antiseptic, a cough suppressant, and a decongestant, you couldn't do much better than **onions** and **garlic.** These potent sulfurous veggies ease coughs and congestion. If you're brave enough, combine two finely chopped onions with two tablespoons of honey. Cover and let it sit overnight and then take a tablespoon to ease congestion.

Elderberries are good antimicrobial foods, meaning you don't need to know if you have a bacterial or fungal or viral infection, because it will help knock them all out.

All sorts of hot peppers—**jalapeños, chilies, habaneros**—help break up congestion, so go for them! They're also a good source of vitamin C, a natural antibiotic. Spicy-hot foods like **mustard greens, horseradish**, and **kohlrabi** from the cabbage family, as well as those served piping hot, are very effective at easing congestion.

Thyme is used throughout Europe to stimulate immune function and clear mucus from the lungs and airways.

BRUISES

YOUR GARDEN RX: cabbage leaves, blueberries, citrus fruits, tomatoes, sweet peppers, arugula, parsley

Bruises are usually the result of an injury that breaks the tiny blood vessels under your skin without breaking the skin. The purple and blue marks are actually pooled blood that will in time be reabsorbed by your body.

Strengthening your blood vessels and the elastic-like collagen in your body will help prevent bruising or make bruising less likely should you have an injury. If you have chronic bruising and fragile skin, you may have a vitamin C deficiency, so C-rich foods will help.

YOUR GARDEN TO THE RESCUE

Blueberries, citrus fruits, tomatoes, and **sweet peppers** are all rich in vitamin C and will help strength the connective tissue to prevent or minimize bruising.

Cabbage and **arugula** leaves and crushed **parsley** cooked in wine are time-honored remedies for bruises when they're applied as poultices to speed the healing process and disperse the pooled blood beneath the skin. In addition, arugula and other green leafy vegetables are good sources of vitamin K, a nutrient that may be deficient in people who are prone to easy bruising.

BURNS

YOUR GARDEN RX: chamomile, onions, garlic, cucumber, apples
We don't easily forget the pain of a burn, which can last from minutes to weeks. While there is little we can do to prevent burns except—duh—be a little more careful, accidents do happen. The immediate first aid for a burn is cool water to stop the burning action through the layers of skin. Over the long term, while it is healing, you'll want to keep the skin clean and moist.

If the burn is serious, you'll actually see the layers of skin repairing themselves.

YOUR GARDEN TO THE RESCUE

In the short term, you'll be looking for nice, cool things to put on your burn. **Cucumbers** immediately come to mind, especially if you've got some in the fridge. They'll not only soothe the sore skin; they'll draw out the heat.

Poultices of **onions** or **garlic** can help cleanse the burn and prevent infection. There is some evidence that onions may even reduce scarring, and garlic may help regenerate the damaged skin.

Apples can also help heal burns with a gel-like substance called pectin (it's what makes jelly jell). Just rubbing an apple slice on the burn can help healing, but it may not do much for pain.

CANCER PREVENTION

YOUR GARDEN RX: garlic, onions, broccoli, berries (all types), beans, chili peppers, pumpkin seeds, rosemary, red grapes, tomatoes, celery, cauliflower, cabbage, Brussels sprouts
There is abundant evidence that a diet rich in all kinds of fruits and vegetables can prevent most types of cancers. That's because as we age, we literally start to get a little rusty. Free-radical oxygen molecules attack

our cells, much like rust on a car bumper, and mess up the DNA codes that once prompted cells to divide into perfect copies of their parent cells. Among other things, this can cause cancer. Almost all fruits and vegetables are rich sources of antioxidants, so think of them as scrubbing that rust off the bumper.

The National Cancer Institute estimates that one-third of all cancer deaths are related to diet in some way.

There are some powerhouse fruits and vegetables and herbs that not only are study-proven to prevent a wide variety of cancers; some can even slow the growth of existing cancers.

YOUR GARDEN TO THE RESCUE

Garlic is often called a superfood because of its multitude of health-giving, even life-saving nutrients. One substance found in garlic, s-allyl-cysteine, stops cells from becoming cancerous and others, like sulfides, actually stops already cancerous cells from dividing, working in ways that are similar to some chemotherapy agents but nontoxic. Study after study has shown that people who eat the most garlic have the lowest rates of a variety of cancers, including stomach, colon, and liver.

Onions have many of the same sulfur compounds as garlic, with the addition of fructo-oligosaccharides that have a unique ability to knock out bacteria that may cause certain types of gastrointestinal cancers. Onions can slow the growth of breast, colorectal, and oral-cavity cancers.

Broccoli and other cruciferous vegetables like **cauliflower, cabbage**, and **Brussels sprouts** are rich sources of indole-3-carbinols, substances that neutralize the effects of harmful estrogens. That makes them particularly important in preventing breast and other hormonally related cancers.

The sulforaphane in these vegetables deactivates those dastardly free radicals and helps prevent colon and rectal cancers.

Red grapes are a rich source of resveratrol and ellagic acid, among the most potent antioxidants known. These substances can wipe out the enzymes that encourage cancer cell growth and prevent your immune system from correcting the wild cell growth.

Beans are a low-fat superfood, rich in a variety of nutrients, fiber, and protease inhibitors that have been proven to keep normal cells from turning cancerous and prevent cancer cells from growing. Go for the darker-colored dried varieties, like black beans and kidney beans.

Chili peppers like **jalapeños** contain a chemical, capsaicin, that can neutralize cancer-causing nitrosamines and may help prevent gastrointestinal cancers.

Berries of all kinds, especially **blueberries**, are good sources of cell-protecting ellagic acid. Not only does ellagic acid prevent cellular changes that can lead to cancer, it reduces free-radical damage and help sweep carcinogens out of your system.

Rosemary can help increase the activity of detoxification enzymes and even slow the development of both breast and skin tumors.

Tomatoes are a source of carotenoids that offer so many health benefits. Among these substances is lycopene, which has been study proven to reduce the risk of breast, prostate, pancreatic, and colorectal cancers. One study shows that lycopene actually kills mouth cancer cells.

Celery has a unique type of phenolic acids that actually block the action of prostaglandins, hormone-like substances that encourage the growth of cancer cells.

CANKER SORES, COLD SORES

YOUR GARDEN RX: chamomile, sage, raspberries, beets, tomatoes, sprouts, strawberries, green peppers
Canker sores or cold sores can have a variety of causes, including the herpes simplex virus, which is usually the culprit in the ones that occur outside your lips.

The ones inside your mouth usually have one of three causes:

- Irritation from spicy or rough-textured foods
- Injuries (like biting your lip or tongue, or problems with dental appliances)
- Stress or chewing the inside of your mouth

If you have a sore caused by the herpes virus, you probably already know that there is no known cure for herpes. However, research shows that foods with significant amounts of the amino acid lysine may diminish the number of herpes outbreaks.

If your sore is due to injury or irritation caused by food or stress, the good news is that it will probably heal on its own in a few days. You can speed healing by swishing a teaspoon of unrefined sea salt in eight ounces of warm water in your mouth two or three times a day.

YOUR GARDEN TO THE RESCUE

If it is an external sore: Look for foods rich in lysine and low in arginine to contain the herpes virus. **Beets, tomatoes**, and most types of **sprouts** are good suppressors of the herpes virus, and eating them may diminish the number outbreaks.

You'll want to avoid arginine-rich foods, including chocolate, nuts, caffeine, and products made with white flour, because they aggravate the herpes virus.

RX from Outside Your Garden

For internal or external sores: a milk compress (five seconds on, five seconds off for five minutes, three or four times a day) may help dry up a canker sore or cold sore.

You'll also do well with immune system–enhancing foods rich in vitamin C, like **strawberries** and **green peppers**.

If the sore is inside your mouth: **Chamomile** tea is a good source of natural painkillers and has a drawing property that can help dry up mouth sores quickly. Raspberry root bark or leaf (dried or fresh in a tea) is not only a natural painkiller, it's got three "anti's:" it's antiseptic, anti-inflammatory, and antiviral. **Sage** laves have drawing properties that can help dry up those inflamed mouth sores that you seem to bite over and over again.

CARPAL TUNNEL SYNDROME (ALSO SEE HYPOTHYROIDISM)

YOUR GARDEN RX: **Pumpkin and sunflower seeds, walnuts**

Carpal tunnel syndrome is an inflammatory condition that results from repetitive use of the metacarpals ("fingers" in lay language) and constriction in the nerve tunnel that runs from the fingers through the wrist. It's a disease of our times because it is common among people who use computers and do a great deal of keyboarding. Carpal tunnel syndrome can also be a symptom of hypothyroidism.

YOUR GARDEN TO THE RESCUE

Essential fatty acids, like those you find in nuts and seeds like **pumpkin, sunflower**, and **walnuts** and in their oils, help counteract inflammatory prostaglandins, minimizing the swelling and relieving the symptoms.

If you use a computer for hours a day, be sure your posture is good (back straight and chin roughly parallel to the floor) and your wrist in neutral position (more or less straight) when you're typing.

RX from Outside Your Garden

Flaxseed and flaxseed oil are potent sources of essential fatty acids and can help reduce the inflammation of carpal tunnel, although you're unlikely to be growing flaxseed in your garden.

CELIAC DISEASE

YOUR GARDEN RX: **spinach, kale, collards, Swiss chard, potatoes, beans, cantaloupe, tomatoes, sweet potatoes, sunflower seeds**

Celiac disease is a hereditary disease that is characterized by sensitivity to gluten in wheat, barley, rye, and some other cereal grains, causing severe gastrointestinal upsets.

Happily, modern medicine and natural medicine are on the same page about this one: Avoid products containing gluten, including bread, cakes, pastries, etc. This rigorous dietary constraint has become easier in recent years with a plethora of gluten-free foods on the market due to the increased awareness of the problem of gluten intolerance as well as higher awareness of the proper treatment of the problem by people who have intolerances, including celiac disease.

Many people who have celiac disease are also lactose intolerant, which means they cannot properly digest dairy products.

YOUR GARDEN TO THE RESCUE

If you have celiac disease, you'll be happy to know that virtually anything you grow in your garden (unless you're into growing wheat) is gluten-free and you can eat as much of it as you want. While there is no known cure for celiac disease, it is manageable.

Deficiencies in vitamins A, D, E, and K, as well as iron and magnesium, are common among people with celiac disease, so search out foods that have good levels of these essential nutrients for the best results.

Spinach is at the top of that list, as an excellent source of vitamins A, C, and K as well as iron. Most leafy greens like **kale, collards**, and **Swiss chard** are nearly as good. **Potatoes**, and especially potato flours as an alternative to wheat flours, are usually well tolerated by people with celiac disease.

Cantaloupe and **tomatoes** are great sources of vitamin C, and **sweet potatoes** are a great source of vitamin A.

Sunflower seeds are a good source of vitamin E that you can grow in your garden.

BONUS FROM YOUR GARDEN

Did you know that the sun is your best (and cheapest) source of vital vitamin D? Just getting out and weeding your garden for 15 minutes a day—without sunscreen on your arms, shoulders, and legs—will let you absorb enough ultraviolet B (UVB) rays to manufacture all the vitamin D you need.

CHRONIC FATIGUE SYNDROME AND FIBROMYALGIA

YOUR GARDEN RX: garlic, cabbage, mustard greens, potatoes, rose hips
Chronic fatigue syndrome (CFS) is a terrible hodgepodge of symptoms that leave you feeling utterly drained.

If bed rest does not improve the exhaustion for a period of six months or more, your doctor may be able to arrive at an official diagnosis. Many CFS sufferers spend years going from doctor to doctor before they are diagnosed.

Symptoms can include weakness and muscle pain (also symptoms of fibromyalgia, characterized mainly by extreme sensitivity at certain muscle trigger points), impaired memory, headaches, insomnia, and exhaustion following physical exercise, if the exhaustion lasts more than twenty-four hours. In addition to the food recommendations included in this section, look for more advice among the entries for other symptoms you are experiencing.

If you do get a definitive diagnosis, conventional medicine will often treat you with antidepressants and behavioral counseling, since that is about all conventional or allopathic medicine has to offer.

YOUR GARDEN TO THE RESCUE

Your garden has much to offer in terms of relief. **Garlic** has been shown to reduce the symptoms of fatigue from physical exertion and it seems to work for people with CFS as well. Increasing your consumption of foods rich in various forms of B vitamins, like **cabbage, broccoli, cauliflower**, and **spinach**, will help.

Potatoes and other foods high in potassium and magnesium can help relieve muscle pain and fatigue.

Low levels of a "feel good" brain chemical called dopamine can cause fatigue, so eating **mustard greens** and **watercress**, which are good sources of tyrosine, the amino acid from which dopamine is made by your body, can help relieve the fatigue and low energy.

Research shows that vitamin C is a factor in reducing fatigue, so eating a variety of foods rich in vitamin C can improve your stamina. **Rose hips**, those budlike remainders of roses after they have bloomed, have very high vitamin C levels. You can dry them and make a make a wonderful tart tea from them. Other C-rich foods are **strawberries, tomatoes, cantaloupe**, and **citrus fruits**.

RX from Outside Your Garden

Many people with CFS have low blood pressure. Unrefined sea salt is a good source of the minerals you need, including sodium, to bring your blood pressure and your energy back to normal. Also, you're probably not growing bananas in your garden, but a potassium-rich banana a day can keep the muscle pain away.

COLDS/FLU

YOUR GARDEN RX: **elderberries, hot peppers, bell peppers, butternut squash, cherries, garlic, onions, mushrooms, sage, echinacea**

We all know there is no cure for the common cold and most of us know that colds and flu are caused by viruses, against which antibiotics are useless and may even be dangerous in the long term. Overuse of antibiotics can diminish their effects when you really need them to fight a serious infection, for example.

Doctors tell you to rest, drink lots of fluids, and wait for a week or two for the cold or flu to pass. All of that is good advice, but there are foods that will strengthen your immune system so you aren't as likely to get colds or flu, as well as foods and herbs that will help shorten the duration and soften the symptoms when you do get sick.

YOUR GARDEN TO THE RESCUE

Let's start with strengthening your immune system to prevent colds and flu. **Onions** and **garlic** are among our best sources of immune system–strengthening compounds, including sulfur and allicin. Keep colds and flu away with these powerhouse nutrients.

Foods rich in selenium are also important immune system strengtheners, although most of them are meat and seafoods. If you're growing

mushrooms in your basement, you've got a jump start on beating seasonal colds and flu.

Echinacea has been shown to be helpful in strengthening the immune system, although some studies question its effectiveness.

If you've already got a cold or flu, **hot peppers** and **chili peppers** will help ease the congestion in your head and chest. Some of us masochistically enjoy drinking cayenne pepper tea with lemon and maybe a little bit of honey when a cold hits.

Elderberries are a powerhouse of natural antiviral compounds, so load up on them if a cold or flu has got you down and out. They reduce inflammation and the muscle aches so common with the flu. In addition, elderberry syrup is an excellent cough remedy. If you grow elderberries (a simple task), dry a few against the winter cold season. Like any other dried produce, dried elderberries can be reconstituted by pouring boiling water over them and allowing them to stand for 10–15 minutes.

Sage tea soothes sore throats and calms coughs.

Of course, vitamin C–rich foods are an essential part of your arsenal against colds and flu. **Red** and **green bell peppers, butternut squash**, and **cherries** (and all **citrus fruits**, of course) are among the best sources of this vitamin, which has antiviral properties.

RX from Outside Your Garden

Dark chocolate (oh, yes!) contains theobromine, an excellent cough suppressant. This is enough to make you happy even if you have a miserable cold.

COLITIS (ALSO SEE IRRITABLE BOWEL SYNDROME)

YOUR GARDEN RX: **leeks, cabbage, brocolli, potatoes, squash, pumpkin, zucchini, pears**

Colitis, sometimes called ulcerative colitis, affects bowel function and, true to its name, can cause bleeding ulcers in the colon and rectum. It is often accompanied by severe stomach cramps and violent, bloody diarrhea.

Colitis sufferers usually have periodic flare-ups followed by periods of normal bowel function.

The cause of colitis is unknown, although it often follows an episode of food poisoning or a bacterial infection, oddly enough, in people who have been taking antibiotics to treat an infection.

Colitis can also be caused by a loss of blood supply to the bowel, most frequently because of a contortion of the bowel itself.

Diet is an essential means of treating colitis, and most people with the disease have learned that certain foods tend to trigger flare-ups or worsen episodes already in progress. The most common trigger foods are wheat, sugar, and dairy products, so eliminating them from your diet is likely to have a positive effect.

YOUR GARDEN TO THE RESCUE

You'll want to avoid harsh, acidic, or spicy foods for obvious reasons.

Leeks can stop intestinal cramping, gas, and bloating. They have mucilage that coats and soothes the irritated bowel lining.

Cabbage and other cruciferous vegetables like **broccoli** have the same intestinal soothing effect. Cabbage has specifically been used to heal ulcers, as have **squash, pumpkin**, and **zucchini**.

The mild comforting effect of **potatoes** can help soothe an irritated bowel. Potato juice has traditionally been used as a folk remedy for all type of ulcers.

Pectin and fiber in **pears** can help stop diarrhea, and the cooling tannins can calm an irritated digestive tract.

These foods should be gently poached, perhaps in chicken broth for flavor, without added spices.

CONJUNCTIVITIS

YOUR GARDEN RX: blueberry, bilberry, cucumber, chamomile

Conjunctivitis is an inflammation of the conjunctiva, which is the surface of the eye and the inner surface of the eyelid. It is often caused by a viral infection but can occasionally be the result of an allergic reaction or a bacterial infection. It is very painful and usually results in an extreme sensitivity to light. There may be a yellow-green mucous discharge from the eye if the inflectional is bacterial.

Modern medicine often treats conjunctivitis with antibiotics, although that will be ineffective if the cause is viral or allergic. Cold compresses and even cool eyewashes can help ease the inflammation.

YOUR GARDEN TO THE RESCUE

Blueberries and **bilberries**, mashed and steeped in water and strained, are a traditional treatment for conjunctivitis. They are rich in vitamins A and C and are a potent source of antioxidants that reduce inflammation and help strengthen the immune response to viral and bacterial invaders.

Cucumbers, especially if they have been in the refrigerator, can be sliced and placed on your eyes for cooling relief. While we're still thinking "cool," a mild wash of **chamomile** tea can help ease the pain.

CONSTIPATION

YOUR GARDEN RX: apples, dried beans, berries, rhubarb, squash
We've all experienced constipation from time to time. The cramping and bloating that accompany the inability to move your bowels can be tiring as well as painful.

Here's one place where conventional medicine and natural medicine agree: Fiber, fiber, and more fiber plus lots and lots of water are the best remedies for constipation. Modern medicine diverges by often advising moving things along with stool softeners, laxatives, and even enemas.

It's best to avoid laxatives and stool softeners, which can actually impair the return of normal bowel function and, with long-term use, leave you dependent on them. Let nature take her course. Unless you have a serious disease situation, water and fiber and light exercise will give you results in a day or two.

YOUR GARDEN TO THE RESCUE

Almost all fruits and vegetables are good sources of fiber and water, so enjoy your produce. **Apples** may be your best friends, because they have both soluble and insoluble fiber in the flesh and the skin.

Dried beans are among the best-known sources of fiber, and if you're concerned about the gassiness that accompanies bean eating, add a little ginger when you cook them.

In addition to providing fiber, all kinds of **berries** prevent bile acid from converting to carcinogenic compounds, thus promoting good health on several fronts. **Elderberries** are among the most potent natural laxatives, but **blackberries, blueberries**, and **strawberries** are also good.

Rhubarb is an excellent source of insoluble fiber with a natural laxative effect. Dark green **winter squashes** also have many of the same effects.

RX from Outside Your Garden

Dehydration is a frequent cause of constipation, so drink lots and lots of water. To determine how much water you need, experts recommend dividing your body weight by two and multiplying by an ounce a day. In other words, if you weigh 150 pounds, you need at least 75 ounces of water every day.

COPD (CHRONIC OBSTRUCTIVE PULMONARY DISEASE)

YOUR GARDEN RX: **winter squash, green peppers, strawberries, carrots, sweet potatoes, walnuts, sunflower seeds**

COPD encompasses emphysema, chronic bronchitis, and chronic asthmatic bronchitis, diseases characterized by damage to the airways and air sacs in the lungs that cause breathing to become difficult. COPD is most often caused by cigarette smoking. Symptoms usually worsen over time. Conventional medicine treats COPD with steroids.

YOUR GARDEN TO THE RESCUE

There is a wide range of delicious **winter squashes**, like Hubbard and butternut, and all of them are rich in lung-healthy vitamin C and beta carotene. Toxicologists at the EPA confirm that people with the highest levels of vitamin C in their blood have the lowest risk of lung diseases. That's because vitamin C is a strong antioxidant that helps neutralize lung damage caused by environmental toxins like air pollution and cigarette smoke. It may also slow the progression of COPD.

Other foods high in C like **green peppers** and **strawberries**, and, of course, citrus fruits, will help protect you.

Carrots and **sweet potatoes** are other good sources of beta carotene.

Pump up your consumption of nuts, like **walnuts**, and seeds, like **sunflower seeds**, for the vitamin E that helps prevent oxidative damage as well.

COUGH

YOUR GARDEN RX: elderberries, chili peppers, horseradish, peppermint
We've all experienced wracking coughs that seem to linger on long past the end of a common cold and keep us from sleeping. That's probably why we spend billions of dollars a year trying to quiet those pesky coughs.

While coughs are usually part of the annoyance of a cold, they can also be a sign of bronchitis or sinusitis.

YOUR GARDEN TO THE RESCUE

Gargle some strong peppermint tea and take advantage of its natural cough suppressants and irritant soothers.

Elderberries are among my favorite remedies for colds and whenever my immune system needs a boost, but they are equally effective against coughs when you make them into a berry-sweetened syrup, which is also effective against allergies and sinus inflammation.

If you're brave, try some **chili peppers** to help thin the mucus and reduce chest congestion. If you're even braver, try some **horseradish** for its phlegm-thinning properties.

RX from Outside Your Garden

Try any of these options to find relief from a cough:

- Suck on a clove
- Take a spoonful of honey
- Brew a cup of ginger tea
- Sip a bowl of chicken soup
- Best of all, eat a piece of good dark chocolate

CROHN'S DISEASE

YOUR GARDEN RX: potatoes, sweet potatoes, squash, carrots, beets, beans, applesauce

Similar to ulcerative colitis, Crohn's disease most often affects the lower end of the small intestine and results in many of the same symptoms as colitis: diarrhea and abdominal cramping. Crohn's sometimes causes intestinal blockages, which can be life threatening.

People with Crohn's are usually advised to avoid high-fiber and fatty foods. Because there may be a food sensitivity component to Crohn's, it's a good idea to isolate certain foods and see if they cause a flare-up. The most common triggers are wheat and dairy products.

People with Crohn's may have vitamin and mineral deficiencies because of chronic diarrhea.

YOUR GARDEN TO THE RESCUE

Most people with Crohn's are advised to avoid raw fruits and vegetables. Gentle foods like baked **potatoes** (avoid the fiber-rich skins during a flare-up), **sweet potatoes**, and steamed **squash** are nutrient-packed and gentle on the digestive tract, as are **carrots, beets**, and **green** and **yellow beans**.

Applesauce will also give you the pectin that soothes the mucosa of the intestinal tract.

CUTS, SORES

YOUR GARDEN RX: garlic, thyme, plantain, spinach

Your first concern when you get a cut is to stop the bleeding; the second is to prevent infection; and the third is to promote healing.

For the most part, you don't need to succumb to the doctor's wish to give you antibiotics and/or a tetanus shot. That's not necessary in most cases, unless there is contact with rusty metal or legitimate reason to fear serious bacterial contamination.

Generally, keep the cut clean and covered and it will heal in a few days.

Fortunately, your garden offers many ways to clean and heal that cut.

YOUR GARDEN TO THE RESCUE

Here we go with **garlic** again: It's one of nature's most powerful antiseptics, so putting a garlic poultice on the cut will help draw out dirt and bacteria. **Thyme** and **plantain** (that wide-leafed weedy thing that is probably growing in your driveway or somewhere in your yard) are also powerful antibacterials.

For the healing process itself, you can't beat several big spinach salads for the increased zinc you'll get to help remodel your skin.

> ### RX from Outside Your Garden
>
> Honey is a great antibacterial and can act as a natural bandage, since it will seal the cut as it dries.

CYSTS (CERVICAL AND OVARIAN)

YOUR GARDEN RX: onions, garlic, blueberries, milk thistle, dandelion leaves, burdock, yellow dock

Cervical and ovarian cysts are most often harmless growths. Ovarian cysts can grow inside or outside the ovaries. Cervical cysts are just as they might seem—small pockets, usually of mucus, that grow inside the cervix.

YOUR GARDEN TO THE RESCUE

Foods that help detoxify the body can be helpful in reducing the incidence of ovarian and cervical cysts. **Onions, garlic**, and **blueberries** are among the most potent detoxifying foods, and the antimicrobial properties of onions and garlic may also help stop any secondary infection. Detoxifying herbs, such as **milk thistle,** can also be helpful. You're not likely to be actively cultivating so-called "weeds" like **dandelions**, **burdock**, and **yellow dock**, but you'll undoubtedly find these helpful detoxifiers nearby.

DEHYDRATION

YOUR GARDEN RX: watermelon, cantaloupe, pears, peaches, tomatoes
If you're dehydrated, you need water, plain and simple.

Dehydration can cause a wide variety of health problems, including muscle cramping, weakness, headache, and in serious cases, convulsions, heart failure, kidney failure, and death.

In severe cases, you must be hospitalized and your fluid balance restored intravenously.

If you are dehydrated, you need to increase your water consumption until the symptoms disappear and then adopt a regimen of drinking water daily. If plain water is distasteful to you, add a little squeeze of lemon, a sprig of peppermint, or a bit of ginger.

YOUR GARDEN TO THE RESCUE

While water is always the best remedy, lots of watery vegetables and fruits and juices will help you get back the deficit and even help replace some of your lost electrolytes.

Think about watery foods like **watermelon, cantaloupe, pears, peaches**, and **tomatoes**. When you add in the A and C vitamins and rich mineral content, these foods will help rehydrate you and they will help keep you hydrated.

DEPRESSION

YOUR GARDEN RX: kale, spinach, dried beans, mushrooms, sunflower seeds, oregano, garlic, onions

There are several types of depression, with the following being the most common:

- Mild moodiness from time to time
- Winter blues (often related to vitamin D shortfalls in winter)
- Holiday- or anniversary-related sadness, especially in remembrance of times past and loved ones who are no longer here
- Full-blown moderate or even major depression

While there are definitely psychological components of depression, most clinical depression is caused by shortfalls in certain brain chemicals called neurotransmitters. You've probably heard of serotonin, dopamine, and norepinephrine, the Big Three "feel-better" neurotransmitters. Low levels of any of these can cause depression, cravings, addiction, obesity, insomnia, and other unpleasant health side effects.

Modern medicine likes to prescribe antidepressants for just about anyone who complains of sadness, despite the fact that they don't work at all for half the people who take them. There often is a price for those who do get positive results, in the form of serious side effects.

Fortunately, your garden has several good answers, and natural medicine has even more.

YOUR GARDEN TO THE RESCUE

A number of nutrients, including B and C vitamins and selenium, give your body the building blocks to manufacture the neurotransmitters that will lift your mood.

Green leafy vegetables like **kale, spinach,** and dark green **lettuces** (not iceberg; that has almost no nutritional value), **sunflower seeds**, and **dried beans** are excellent sources of vitamin B6, also known as folate, the building block for serotonin. This is especially important if you are taking folate-depleting birth control pills or hormone replacement.

Brazil nuts are by far the best source of selenium, a mineral that appears to play a key role in depression. **Mushrooms,** which you can grow in your basement, are among the few vegetable sources of selenium. **Oregano** has much the same effect.

Although **onions** and **garlic** are commonly associated with relief from depression, they contain substances that act just like the old-time antidepressant medications called MAO-inhibitors, which often are more effective than the newer medicines.

RX from Outside Your Garden

Chocolate has more than 300 brain-altering compounds that can raise your spirits. No wonder we love it so much! If you haven't gotten the message by now, I love chocolate and I am very glad that it is good for us!

DIABETES

YOUR GARDEN RX: **dark green leafy veggies, dried beans, green beans, onions and garlic, sweet potatoes, blueberries, sunflower and pumpkin seeds, nuts, avacadoes**

Diabetes is one of the most widespread and insidious diseases known to the modern world. Type 2 diabetes, the most common form, generally begins in adulthood, although it is becoming disturbingly common in teenagers and even preteens. That's because 95 percent of people with Type 2 diabetes are obese.

With today's epidemic of obesity, it's not surprising that more and people will be affected by this disease, which comes from the body's inability to use the insulin it produces to balance blood sugar from our diets.

It also opens you to high risk of other serious diseases, including heart disease, kidney failure, macular degeneration (an eye condition that can cause blindness), and circulatory problems that can lead to amputations.

Conventional medicine chooses to treat most people with Type 2 diabetes as though they have already had a heart attack, largely because their risk of a heart attack is very high, about triple that of nondiabetics.

Diabetes demands strict attention to diet and restricting the intake of simple sugars, including excessive amounts of fruit. It pretty much bans fruit juice altogether.

Today's dietary guidelines for people with diabetes no longer prohibit sugary foods, instead emphasizing a healthy diet and exercise program that is much more realistic than complete avoidance of simple sugars.

Exercise is very important because the energy used by muscles enhances absorption of insulin and makes it better able to balance blood sugar.

Conventional medicine treats diabetes with a wide range of pharmaceuticals. People with diabetes often take multiple medications to control blood sugar as well as drugs to control cholesterol levels and blood pressure, and to support the hearts, kidneys, and eyes.

There is no cure for diabetes. However, choosing the healthiest possible lifestyle can lower your need for medications, and perhaps even eliminate the need for some as you begin to control your blood sugar more effectively.

Weight control is at the heart of almost all diabetes treatment plans, since so many people with diabetes are obese.

YOUR GARDEN TO THE RESCUE

Because weight control is probably your goal, almost everything in your garden is good for you. Remember, you'll need to limit the intake of fruit (most docs say no more than two servings a day) and some starchy veggies like potatoes.

But you can load up on low-sugar, high-energy foods like dark green leafy veggies (**kale, collards, dark green lettuces, spinach**).

Foods high in fiber, like our favorite **dried beans**, slow down the digestive process and ration the entry of sugars into your system. The high fiber content in **sweet potatoes** and their unique levels of chlorogenic acid also help control blood sugars.

Onions are great for diabetics because they have chromium, antioxidants, and flavonoids that can give you major blood sugar reduction when you eat two or more ounces per day. They can also help raise your metabolic rate when eaten raw.

Garlic, another perennial favorite, helps lower blood sugar and encourages the pancreas to produce more insulin.

All kinds of **nuts** and **avocados** contain good fats that help lower insulin resistance.

RX from Outside Your Garden

Many studies show that cinnamon helps lower blood sugar. Choose complex carbohydrates that absorb their sugars slowly into your bloodstream, such as brown rice and baked goods made with whole grains (not just whole wheat).

DIARRHEA

YOUR GARDEN RX: **apples, potatoes, carrots, garlic, onions, leeks**

Almost everyone is affected by diarrhea from time to time. Although it's most commonly caused by a virus or food sensitivity, it can also be caused by a bacteria attached to food (food poisoning).

Most cases of diarrhea disappear in a day or two without treatment because we have large colonies of helpful bacteria in our digestive tracts that can fight off pathogens without too much trouble.

However, diarrhea caused by other illnesses (colitis or inflammatory bowel disease, for example) or episodes that last more than a few days can be serious, primarily because you're losing large amounts of fluid from your system and you're at risk of dehydration. Children are especially vulnerable to dehydration from diarrhea and can be at risk of serious illness in as little as one day.

YOUR GARDEN TO THE RESCUE

Avoid most raw fruits and vegetables for a few days and go with lightly steamed gentle veggies (asparagus, peeled zucchini, green beans, peas), or a baked **potato** and maybe a little homemade **applesauce** for the pectin that helps control diarrhea.

Carrots can help soothe an irritated digestive tract and help replace vital nutrients lost due to diarrhea.

Garlic, onions, and **leeks** are natural sources of probiotics that naturally balance your out-of-whack intestinal microorganisms.

RX from Outside Your Garden

Try the BRAT diet: Banana, (brown) Rice, Applesauce, and (whole grain) Toast

DIVERTICULITIS

YOUR GARDEN RX: apples, dried beans, chamomile, peppermint, thyme
Sometimes small particles of food become trapped in the naturally occurring diverticula or little pouchlike projections in the large intestine. When this happens, the diverticula become inflamed and can cause a painful episode called diverticulitis. Constipation often goes hand-in-hand with diverticulitis.

Seeds, nuts, and small particles of food like corn, tomato seeds, and celery strings are most likely to be trapped in the diverticula, so it's a good idea to avoid them if you have experienced this problem.

In general, people with diverticulitis need a high-fiber diet, and for that it's only a short trip to your garden.

YOUR GARDEN TO THE RESCUE

Apples may be your number one tool against diverticulitis because they are sources of pectin and soluble and insoluble fiber, an excellent pairing to soothe the irritated digestive tract and to usher food through your intestines without causing problems.

Other high-fiber foods, like **dried beans** (cooked with a carrot and perhaps an onion to help keep down the gas and bloating) will also help in the long run after an acute attack has passed.

Herbs that soothe our digestive tract can also offer relief, including **peppermint, chamomile**, and **thyme**. Peppermint has loads of anti-inflammatory compounds, painkillers, and sedatives. It should be part of your garden and part of everyone's medicinal arsenal.

DRY SKIN

YOUR GARDEN RX: sunflower and pumpkin seeds, carrots, sweet potatoes, green peppers, strawberries, citrus fruits
Dry skin is most often caused by overexposure to sun, dry indoor air, or a diet too low in fat. We all need the good fats that come from seed and nut oils. Dry skin can be one of the first signs that we're short on good fats. That shortage can have far-reaching consequences, including heart disease and stroke.

Thyroid disease and other endocrine disorders can also cause dry skin, so if there isn't a logical explanation for your dry skin, you might want to have your thyroid function checked.

RX from Outside Your Garden

Avocados are an excellent form of skin-healthy fat, as are fish like salmon, mackerel, and tuna.

YOUR GARDEN TO THE RESCUE

Pumpkin and sunflower seeds contain healthy oils, and they're a good source of skin-healthy vitamin E. If you're lucky enough to be able to grow nuts, you'll find their natural oils help to moisturize your skin as well.

Vitamin C is an internal skin moisturizer often recommended by dermatologists, so C-rich foods like **green peppers, strawberries**, and **citrus fruits** will certainly help.

Carrots and **sweet potatoes** are also good sources of beta carotene, a form of vitamin A with strong antioxidant properties that helps protect your skin from sun damage.

EAR INFECTIONS

YOUR GARDEN RX: garlic, onions, oregano
Ear infections can have a wide range of causes, although the vast majority are caused by a cold virus that migrates into the eustachian tubes in the ears. Ear infections are most common in children, but adults can also get earaches and ear infections from viruses as well as from earwax compaction, accumulation of water in the ear (known as swimmer's ear), and unequal pressure due to altitude changes (common among scuba divers). In children, food allergies, particularly to dairy products, can be a factor in recurring ear infections, so it might be worthwhile to eliminate dairy products from the diet to see if the condition improves.

RX from Outside Your Garden

Hydrogen peroxide was Grandma's remedy for earaches, and it continues to serve me and my family well today. Lie on your side with a towel under your head to catch any drips and, using an eyedropper, drip six to eight drops of peroxide into your ear and then wait for two or three minutes. The fizzing sound tells you it's working. The turn over and let it drain out onto a paper towel or tissue. Just for good measure, be sure to treat the other ear, even if you don't have any symptoms.

YOUR GARDEN TO THE RESCUE

Garlic, and **onions** to a somewhat lesser degree, have powerful anti-microbial sulfur compounds that can knock out viruses as well as bacterial and fungal infections, which means you don't have to know what caused the infections to get relief. You can eat your onions and garlic for a systemic inoculation of those antimicrobial benefits or you can squeeze 2–3 cloves of garlic into two tablespoons of olive oil (use a garlic press), let it infuse for a day, strain, warm it slightly, and drop a few droppers-ful into your ear. **Oregano**, which also has excellent antimicrobial properties, can be infused in oil. Strain the oil, warm a small amount, and introduce a few drops into the ear.

ECZEMA

YOUR GARDEN RX: potatoes, chili peppers, dried beans

Eczema is a painful itchy, scaly rash, often one of long duration, most often caused by a food or chemical sensitivity, and sometimes by an overactive immune response like those that cause allergies.

While some of the usual suspects like wheat and dairy allergies can be triggers, eczema may also be a response to eggs, seafood, citrus fruits, bath soaps, laundry detergents, nickel in earrings or other jewelry, wool, animal dander, cold weather, and even stress.

While there can be a variety of symptoms, severe itching is almost always part of eczema, and sufferers often scratch their skin raw. When this happens, secondary infection is a risk.

Conventional medicine usually treats people with eczema with long-term hydrocortisone creams. This is a steroid that can cause serious health problems, so if you can manage your eczema without it, you'll be much better off.

The FDA has also approved two prescription creams, both of which carry the highest level of warnings about health risks.

YOUR GARDEN TO THE RESCUE

Foods high in vitamin B6, also called folates, including **potatoes, chili peppers**, and **dried beans**, can offer relief to eczema sufferers. Keeping your skin hydrated will ease the itching, so the recommendations for dry skin may also help, including sunflower and pumpkin seeds for vitamin E and citrus fruits for vitamin C if you're not sensitive to them.

EYESIGHT DETERIORATION

YOUR GARDEN RX: sweet potatoes, carrots, kale, spinach, melons, tomatoes, potatoes, dried beans, sunflower and pumpkin seeds
Your eyesight might deteriorate for a number of reasons: glaucoma, cataracts, macular degeneration—all of them eye diseases related to aging.

Conventional medicine treats cataracts with surgery and other eye diseases with a variety of pharmaceuticals.

The foods you consume can go a long way toward preventing eye problems and keeping your eyesight healthy.

YOUR GARDEN TO THE RESCUE

Vitamin A is essential for eye health, particularly to improve night vision and to preserve eyesight. Your body converts the beta carotene in foods to vitamin A, so look for a lot of bright orange-colored foods like **carrots, sweet potatoes**, and **cantaloupe** and dark green leafy veggies like **kale** and **spinach** to improve your eyesight. Since most macular degeneration is caused by Type 2 diabetes, low glycemic index **sweet potatoes** are an ideal food for diabetics.

Lycopene, a particular type of carotenoid found in ripe red **tomatoes**, has been proven to prevent cataracts and macular degeneration.

Potatoes and other foods rich in B vitamins will help preserve your eyesight, as will vitamin E–rich **green leafy vegetables** and **sunflower** and **pumpkin seeds.**

FEVER

YOUR GARDEN RX: blackberries, raspberries, blueberries, feverfew, borage, calendula
A fever is nature's way of fighting an infection by raising the body temperature and creating an inhospitable environment for disease-causing microorganisms.

Normal human body temperature is 98.6°F and, while any elevation from that baseline could be considered a fever, treatment isn't required until the temperature exceeds 100.4°F.

It's easy to see why a mild fever is a good thing and probably shouldn't be treated, since the fever indicates that the immune system is doing its job of fighting disease.

However, a fever that gets too high can be dangerous and cause convulsions and delirium. Conventional medicine usually uses aspirin to treat a mild fever and encourages increasing fluid intake. Antibiotics may be used to treat the underlying infection if there is a dangerous fever.

YOUR GARDEN TO THE RESCUE

The common garden **berries**—blackberries, blueberries, and raspberries——are all good sources of vitamin C, which has some natural antibiotic properties. They are also astringent, so they draw out the viral causes of colds, flu, sinusitis, and chest infection that are usually the triggers for a fever. Berries are also a good source of salicylic acid, the pain-relieving and fever-reducing ingredient in aspirin. **Blueberries** are a good source of anthocyanins, which help your body fight infections.

Feverfew has traditionally been used to relieve headaches, but as its name suggests, feverfew is an excellent fever reducer.

Borage is a diuretic and helps increase sweat production, helping cleanse the toxins and dong the work of the fever without the dangers. **Calendula**, with its daisylike flowers, is an astringent and an antiseptic with a rich dose of carotenoids thrown in to help fight infections of all types, even fungal infections.

FLATULENCE

YOUR GARDEN RX: leeks, dill, fennel, peppermint

Gas is a natural product of digestion and *all* of us produce it, no matter how much we may deny it. Gas is actually a sign your digestive system is working correctly.

However, gas can be socially unacceptable. If you eat lots of healthy gas-producing foods like dried beans, cabbage, and cucumbers, don't give up the good foods; just neutralize the gas.

YOUR GARDEN TO THE RESCUE

It may seem counterintuitive, but "stinky" foods in the onion family, particularly leeks, help re-establish the normal intestinal microorganisms to relieve the bloating and cramping that can come from foods that are fermenting in the gut. **Leeks** can also stimulate digestion and ease constipation.

Dill, fennel, and **peppermint** belong to a class of herbs called carminatives, which literally means "anti-gas." All of them ease digestive upsets.

RX from Outside Your Garden

Dandelion roots have wonderful anti-gas properties—most of us can find them right in our own backyards—and yogurt contains the live bacteria to help restore the normal microorganisms that live in your digestive tract.

FOOD POISONING

YOUR GARDEN RX: garlic and onions, mint, raspberry- and blackberry-leaf tea

Food poisoning results from the consumption of contaminated food or water. Despite the media attention to food poisoning that occasionally occurs in restaurants, most cases of food poisoning are caused by improper food handling at home. It's usually characterized by abdominal cramping, vomiting, and diarrhea. Warning: If severe symptoms continue for more than two days or if a group of people who ate or drank the same things become ill, or if the symptoms take place in a child under the age of two, seek medical attention.

YOUR GARDEN TO THE RESCUE

The first remedy is water, which isn't precisely from your garden but is essential to preventing the dehydration that can take place after the vomiting and diarrhea that accompany food poisoning. The antimicrobial powers of **garlic** and **onions** may be able to neutralize the bacteria causing the problem. **Mint** teas will help soothe your stomach and stop the spasms, while **blackberry-** and **raspberry-leaf teas** are not only help-ful in reducing the nausea and diarrhea, but can also help re-establish the mucosal coating in the stomach.

GALLSTONES

YOUR GARDEN RX: radishes, beet greens, dandelion

While gallstones—small lumps in the gallbladder—are not directly related to high cholesterol, they do result from a diet too rich in fat and cholesterol. This "gravel" can cause extreme pain in your right side in the upper or middle abdomen. Conventional medicine usually treats gall stones with drugs that dissolve the stones, or with surgery.

YOUR GARDEN TO THE RESCUE

Radishes are the source of a variety of fat-reducing digestive enzymes that help the gallbladder increase its bile production and soothe irritated bile ducts, preventing the formation of gallstones. **Beet greens** are good sources of betaine, a bile stimulator and simultaneous diluter of bile that helps bile move more easily though the ducts. **Dandelion** leaf tea or greens eaten raw in salads have also been shown to increase bile flow and improve the body's ability to process fat and cholesterol.

GUM DISEASE

YOUR GARDEN RX: strawberries, broccoli, bell peppers, tomatoes, rose hips

Gum inflammation and infection are almost always a result of poor diet. Gum disease is one of the symptoms of scurvy or vitamin C deficiency, which is much more common today than most medical practitioners care to admit, especially among elderly people whose vitamin C consumption and absorption are less than adequate. Gum disease often is the result.

The Standard American Diet (SAD) of processed foods, sugar, and nutritionally void "foods" is largely responsible for our vitamin deficien-cies and the diseases that result from them.

While conventional medicine prefers to treat gum disease with complicated, painful, and expensive dental work and antibiotics, eating enough of the healthy produce from your garden can prevent gum disease and even treat it if you have a mild case.

YOUR GARDEN TO THE RESCUE

Almost everything in your garden will help promote healthier gums, but foods that are high in vitamin C, including **strawberries, broccoli, bell peppers**, and **tomatoes,** will be exceptionally helpful. Drinking a little **rose hip** tea and swishing it around in your mouth before you swallow can also help.

Not only do all of these boost levels of this all-important nutrient in your body, they boost immune system function and act as a natural antibiotic to help fight the infection and inflammation in your gums.

HAIR PROBLEMS

YOUR GARDEN RX: cucumbers, spinach, watermelon, green peppers, dried beans

Hair problems can manifest in a wide variety of ways from brittle, dry hair to thinning and baldness, dandruff, and other scalp issues. While dandruff and scalp rashes are most likely indicative of a skin problem, hair itself is made of keratin, a type of protein.

The main nutrient sources for hair include calcium, magnesium, manganese, silicon, iron, and selenium, as well as vitamins A, B6, and C. If you have hair problems, they may signal a basic nutrient deficiency.

Dry, brittle hair is also a symptom of thyroid disorders and hormonal imbalances, so if basic dietary changes don't improve the situation, ask your doctor about diagnostic tests.

YOUR GARDEN TO THE RESCUE

Cucumbers offer excellent nutrition for your hair, whether you eat them for their abundant mineral content or grate them and wear them on your head for a few minutes to nourish your skin, improve circulation to your scalp, and ease itchiness.

Other foods high in minerals and specifically rich in vitamins to help your hair include **bell peppers** for vitamin C, **spinach** for vitamin A, **watermelon** for vitamin B6, and **dried beans** for biotin and zinc.

HEADACHE, MIGRAINE

YOUR GARDEN RX: garlic, spinach, pumpkin seeds, feverfew, mint, valerian

Migraines are debilitating forms of headache that affect about 10 percent of us and are more common in women than in men. It has long been suggested that there is a hormonal component to migraines, although the headache pattern is highly individual.

Known migraine triggers include:

- Red wine
- Chocolate
- Cheese
- Foods that contain nitrites (such as hot dogs and deli meats)
- Food that contains MSG (monosodium glutamate), especially Chinese food
- Flashing lights
- Weather changes
- Certain odors, particularly perfumes
- Stress

By keeping a journal, you'll be able to get a good handle on your triggers and avoid them.

Yes, stress can cause migraines as well as tension headaches. The primary difference between a migraine and a tension headache is that in addition to the crushing head pain, migraines usually are accompanied by nausea and vomiting and are often signaled by an "aura" or a warning signal that may include disturbances in vision, or specific smells.

Most migraines are believed to have a vascular element, meaning that blood vessels are either contracting or spasming, contributing to the pain.

YOUR GARDEN TO THE RESCUE

Magnesium and vitamin B6 have been shown to stop migraines and perhaps even to prevent them, so eating magnesium- and B6-rich foods like **spinach** and **pumpkin seeds** may help.

Garlic helps thin blood and can stop migraines due to narrowed blood vessels.

Feverfew, mint, and **valerian** can all help when a migraine strikes. Feverfew, traditionally used in Europe for headache relief, has painkilling and anti-inflammatory effects that can help migraine sufferers when other methods fail. Mint will help calm a queasy stomach, and valerian will help you sleep and relieve tension.

> ## RX from Outside Your Garden
>
> Ginger can really relieve the inflammation, the spasms, and the blood vessel constriction and dilation that sparks migraines.

HEADACHE, STRESS

YOUR GARDEN RX: blueberries, tomatoes, bell peppers, cantaloupe, chamomile, catnip

The vast majority (about 90 percent) of all headaches are related to stress and are triggered by tightening of the muscles of your neck and scalp.

Stress headaches can have a number of causes, including the obvious: emotional or mental stress, depression, and fatigue. There can also be less obvious causes: hunger, overexertion, and poor posture.

Chronic tension headaches can occur at regular intervals, sometimes even on a daily basis, and can last anywhere from a few minutes to days on end.

Conventional medicine treats headaches either by ignoring them and suggesting they are "all in your head" (they are—quite literally) or by going overboard with prescription painkillers that can be addicting and have a host of harmful side effects. There are even headaches that are caused by taking too many medications to treat headaches.

YOUR GARDEN TO THE RESCUE

Blueberries are a natural source of pain-relieving salicylic acid, a close cousin to the pain-relieving ingredient in aspirin. **Green peppers, tomatoes,** and **cantaloupes** are also good sources of salicylic acid.

Better yet, try preventing a headache with a cup of calming **chamomile** or **catnip** tea. (I promise the catnip tea won't make you goofy like it does your cat.)

HEARING LOSS

YOUR GARDEN RX: garlic, onions, echinacea, fenugreek, apples, dried beans, sunflower and pumpkin seeds
One-third of all people over 65 have some degree of hearing loss, most commonly caused by arterial plaque buildup in the small blood vessels of the inner ear or impaired nerve conductivity that blocks the transmission of sounds. Hearing loss can also be related to a buildup of earwax or long-term exposure to loud noises. Tinnitus (constant or intermittent ringing, buzzing, or hissing noises) occurs in 85% of people with hearing loss.

YOUR GARDEN TO THE RESCUE

Garlic, onions, apples, and other foods that help lower cholesterol and reduce artery-clogging plaque may also help reduce hearing loss, and a diet rich in these foods and low in saturated fats will almost certainly help prevent high cholesterol and arterial blockages.

A few droppersful of warm **garlic** or **fenugreek** infused olive oil will not only help soften impacted earwax, it may also neutralize microbial infection that can cause hearing loss.

Echinacea will help restore equilibrium and balance and control dizziness. It may also help prevent hearing loss due to infection and the buildup of scar tissue.

Tinnitus has been linked to niacin, zinc, and magnesium shortfalls, so increase your intake of foods high in these nutrients, like **dried beans** and **pumpkin** and **sunflower seeds**.

HEARTBURN

YOUR GARDEN RX: apples, peaches, lettuces and spinach, carrots, broccoli, melons, pears, fennel seeds, chamomile

More formally known as GERD (gastroesophageal reflux disease) is widely believed, even by many doctors, to be caused by excess acid production in the stomach that then splashes up into the esophagus, causing intense pain. In fact, it is not caused by too much acid but by too little acid and by acid in the wrong place for too long. This can happen when the sphincter between the stomach and the esophagus relaxes, allowing the Mexican meal you just scarfed down to splash back up, making you feel like your heart is on fire. In many cases, heartburn and GERD can be caused by food intolerance, most commonly to dairy products.

Heartburn can be a once-in-a-while problem that is painful, but not serious, or it can be a regular plague that can cause severe health problems.

Heartburn is aggravated by alcohol, caffeine, chocolate, and spicy and acidic foods, so if you suffer from occasional heartburn or long-term GERD, avoiding these foods will help. A low-carbohydrate diet will also be helpful, which is why your garden plays such an important role in relieving the pain and the disease.

YOUR GARDEN TO THE RESCUE

Raw veggies including **lettuce, spinach, carrots**, and **broccoli** are the best dietary solutions to heartburn because they are gentle and can help stop the inflammation caused by heartburn. Most doctors recommend lots of salads whether you have occasional heartburn or GERD. Avoid tomatoes and other acidic foods like citrus fruits since they tend to aggravate the condition. **Apples** and **peaches** are soothing fruits as are **melons** and **pears**.

Don't turn to Prilosec! It can actually impair your digestive ability and make digestion dependent on the drug. Instead, you can get quick relief from several herbs, primarily from **fennel seeds** (just chew a teaspoon or so) that help relieve the spasms of the sphincter between the stomach and the esophagus.

The soothing effects of **chamomile** tea can also give you fast relief and relieve the inflammation caused by stomach acid where it doesn't belong.

RX from Outside Your Garden

I'm going to add in ginger here, although since it is tropical, you're unlikely to be able to grow it in your garden, It's a spice with enormous healing power, including helping calm the symptoms of heartburn and stopping the spasming of the sphincter. Make a tea of a one-inch piece of grated gingerroot and find relief.

Again, you're unlikely to be growing **oats** and **wheat** in your garden (although you may decide this would be a fun experiment), but whole grains are a good source of selenium, which is study-proven to relieve GERD.

HEART PROBLEMS

Heart disease, the number one killer in the Western world, is tragic because it is largely preventable.

More people, both men and women (yes, women are just as vulnerable) die of heart disease than any other cause. About 770,000 Americans die every year of heart disease and strokes, more than from cancer and lung disease combined.

Yes, it's true that if your father and grandfather died of heart attacks, that increases your risk. But nothing increases your risk as much as the lifestyle choices you make in terms of diet and exercise. And if your risk is high because of heredity, it's even more important to do everything possible to protect your heart.

If you are obese or have diabetes, your risk of heart disease is huge. Since so many of us are obese *and* have diabetes, our collective risk for all sorts of heart disease is very high.

In general, a diet rich in antioxidant fruits and vegetables has time and again been proven to prevent heart disease and to help reverse the effects of heart disease once it begins, so virtually everything from your garden is good for you.

However, there are specific types of heart disease that can be helped by particular foods, so if you have any of the following conditions, please tailor your diet to address these problems.

ARRHYTHMIA

YOUR GARDEN RX: mustard and turnip greens, chili peppers, dried beans, cantaloupe
Arrhythmia is sometimes called an "electrical storm of the heart." It sounds romantic, but it distinctly is not. Irregular heart rhythms, palpitations, and atrial fibrillation all put you at high risk for a stroke.

Arrhythmia is often linked to a misfiring of the nerves that control the heartbeat. This can be caused by mineral imbalances.

YOUR GARDEN TO THE RESCUE

Look for foods high in potassium and magnesium, such as **cantaloupe** and **mustard** and **turnip greens** and other **green leafy vegetables**, to relax your heart muscle and help normalize your heartbeat.

Foods rich in B vitamins, including **dried beans** and **chili peppers**, will help with nerve conductivity for a steady heartbeat.

ATHEROSCLEROSIS

YOUR GARDEN RX: garlic, apples, blackberries, sunflower and pumpkin seeds, rosemary, purslane

Atherosclerosis, more commonly known as hardening of the arteries, is actually a hardening and thickening of the arteries that supply the heart caused by fat and calcium deposits.

Atherosclerosis is conventionally treated with a battery of prescription drugs that all have a wide range of dangerous side effects, including heart failure. You've no doubt heard of the statin drugs that are supposed to lower cholesterol, which leaves fatty deposits that clog arteries. In fact, those same statin drugs actually impair your body's ability to make coenzyme Q10, an enzyme that, among many other things, reduces the accumulation of oxidized fats in blood vessels, eases high blood pressure, and regulates the rhythm of the heart.

YOUR GARDEN TO THE RESCUE

Garlic has been study-proven to help keep arteries clear and to lower cholesterol levels in people with high cholesterol. The quercetin in garlic is one of the most powerful antioxidants known and is directly linked to the reduction of artery-clogging fats.

High-fiber foods like **apples** can help lower cholesterol and reduce the fatty plaque that clogs arteries.

Vitamins C and E have been shown to stop the clumping of platelets of LDL ("bad") cholesterol in the arteries, so filing up on C-rich foods like **blackberries** and E-rich **pumpkin and sunflower seeds** can help.

Rosemary is another excellent antioxidant. In fact, it was once used to preserve meat—in other words, to prevent oxidation that leads to spoilage. That's what it does for your body, too!

The little-known vegetable **purslane** is the vegetable world's most potent source of blood-thinning omega-3 fatty acids, like those found in heart-healthy salmon, tuna, and mackerel. It's also the source of a perfectly balanced calcium-magnesium ratio.

Purslane leaves are also a good source of anti-inflammatory alpha-lin-olenic acid. Widely regarded as a weed, purslane is a leathery-leaved plant with bright pink flowers. It grows just about everywhere, so look for some at the edges of your yard, presuming you aren't using pesticides on your lawn.

> ### RX from Outside Your Garden
>
> Pomegranate is an exceptionally high-ranking antioxidant that contains substances similar to ACE inhibitors, pharmaceuticals routinely used to treat atherosclerosis.

CHOLESTEROL

YOUR GARDEN RX: garlic, apples, dried beans, carrots, purslane
High levels of total cholesterol, or high levels of LDL or "bad" choles-terol and/or blood fats called triglycerides, are all linked to atherosclerosis and heart attacks.

Cholesterol is a waxy substance that attaches itself to arteries, mainly the larger coronary arteries, and over time can completely block them. Pieces also can break loose and make their way to your heart, causing a heart attack, or to your brain, causing a stroke.

While cholesterol is naturally present in your body, manufactured by the liver, this HDL or "good" cholesterol actually helps usher "bad" cholesterol out of your body. The liver manufactures and removes LDL cholesterol. The danger occurs when we eat a diet too high in satu-rated foods, unbalancing the body's natural cholesterol levels. A diet high in antioxidant foods will help raise HDL cholesterol. Eating too much meat, cheese, butter, eggs, and shellfish is likely to raise your LDL levels.

YOUR GARDEN TO THE RESCUE

The more veggies you eat, the better. The same goes for fruits in somewhat more moderate levels (2–3 servings a day).

Garlic has been specifically proven to help lower total cholesterol levels as well as LDL cholesterol with it sulfur compounds like allicin, which quickly bonds with disease-causing free-radical oxygen molecules and ushers them out of your body.

Apples, with both soluble and insoluble fiber, and **dried beans**, with an abundance of fiber, help literally sweep those unhealthy fats from your system before they can enter your arteries and clog them up.

CONGESTIVE HEART FAILURE

YOUR GARDEN RX: spinach, potatoes, dried beans, asparagus, beets, lettuce, tomatoes
Heart failure happens when your heart stops pumping efficiently. This causes blood to move through your body more slowly than normal and causes your heart to either stretch to try to pump more blood and more oxygen to your tissues or to become thickened and even less effective at beating.

Sometimes the kidneys are affected and fluid builds-up in the tissues, causing fluid buildup in the lungs as well as weakness, dizziness, and/or an irregular heartbeat.

YOUR GARDEN TO THE RESCUE

Since magnesium is key to a strong and steady heartbeat, magnesium-rich foods like **spinach, potatoes**, and **dried beans** may help strengthen your heart.

You'll also want to find some foods that are natural diuretics to help remove fluid from your body, like **asparagus** (which contains asparagine, an alkaloid that improves kidney function) and **beets.** The vitamin C in **tomatoes** helps the kidneys flush out toxins more efficiently. **Lettuce** improves metabolism and helps flush out excess fluids.

HEART ATTACK PREVENTION

YOUR GARDEN RX: tomatoes, cilantro, purslane, spinach, cantaloupe, hawthorn, watermelon, grapefruit
If you are experiencing severe chest pain or any other signs of a heart attack, get to an emergency room immediately. This is where modern medicine excels. It just may save your life.

Heart attacks are caused by a sudden interruption in the blood to your heart, usually due to some type of obstruction in the artery, most often a clot or a piece of atherosclerotic plaque that has broken loose.

You don't have to be a medical expert to know the dangers of a heart attack. Many people do not survive, and those who do have permanent damage to their hearts.

YOUR GARDEN TO THE RESCUE

The lycopene in **tomatoes** has been study-proven to reduce the risk of heart attack dramatically, so keeping tomatoes, **watermelon**, and **grapefruit** in your diet is a good preventive. All of these are good sources of lycopene.

RX from Outside Your Garden

Red wine is widely acknowledged as a good heart attack preventer, provided you drink it in moderation. For women this means a glass a day, and for men, not more than two glasses a day. This amount will reduce the risk of heart attack by half without increasing your risk of alcohol-related diseases.

After a heart attack, you'll want to do everything possible to strengthen your heart muscle and keep it strong with magnesium- and potassium-rich foods, like **spinach** and **cantaloupe.** You'll also want to thin your blood with foods high in vitamin K, such as **cilantro**, and get a natural blood thinning dose of heart-healthy omega-3 fatty acids with **purslane**, a leafy weed-like vegetable.

Hawthorn leaves, flowers, and **berries** act very much like many of the prescription drugs used to treat heart problems, including the ones that open blood vessels and reduce the stress placed on the heart.

HYPERTENSION (HIGH BLOOD PRESSURE)

YOUR GARDEN RX: garlic, spinach, potatoes, onions, sunflower seeds, dried beans

Also known as high blood pressure, hypertension is a silent killer. Millions of Americans have it and don't know they have it, so they don't treat it, placing themselves at risk for heart attack and stroke.

If you have a blood pressure monitor or you make use of one at your local pharmacy, keep a few things in mind:

Blood pressure can change throughout the day. It's usually lowest early in the morning.

Blood pressure goes up when you're moving around. If you're taking a reading, sit still for at least five minutes before measuring it.

Blood pressure responds to stress and illness. When you visit your doctor's office you may experience "white coat hypertension," which is one of the most common forms of elevated blood pressure but is usually temporary. If your doc tells you that your pressure is high, ask for a second reading later in the visit or ask if you can monitor your blood pressure at home over the coming month to determine whether there really is a problem. Many of us get nervous in the doctor's office, and often our pressure will be elevated because we are there for some sort of illness. Long-term stress is another story, and it should be addressed to eliminate one of the most common underlying causes of hypertension.

Your target blood pressure reading should be 120/80. Anything higher could mean you have a problem. Anything significantly lower can indicate an adrenal insufficiency.

YOUR GARDEN TO THE RESCUE

Garlic is a primo vegetable to help relax blood vessels. Allicin, a sulfur compound that gives garlic is odor and its power, has been shown to relax blood vessels and lower blood pressure in addition to providing some other impressive heart-healthy benefits such as improving the body's ability to eliminate "bad" cholesterol and normalizing heart rhythms.

Spinach, sunflower seeds, and **dried beans** (think kidney beans, pintos, and navy beans) are all good sources of magnesium. Your blood vessels are like rubber tubes that are stretched to the max, making them thin and taut. But if the tension on the tube is released, the tube becomes wider and more flexible. Magnesium works just like that in your arteries, helping blood flow more easily and lowering pressure.

Studies show that people who eat magnesium-rich diets have lower blood pressure.

Potatoes (baked or roasted, without butter or sour cream, please!) are an excellent source of potassium, which helps regulate fluid balance in the body. Excess water, fluid buildup, and bloating (usually caused by a sodium-potassium imbalance) put extra pressure on the blood vessels and increase blood pressure. Getting extra potassium from potatoes and the other foods mentioned in this section can help reduce the fluid buildup and normalize blood pressure.

PALPITATIONS

YOUR GARDEN RX: potatoes, spinach, walnuts, dried beans, red grapes, valerian

When your heart starts pounding like crazy, it could mean a number of things, but most likely it means you are stressed or have indulged in a little too much caffeine or alcohol. Palpitations that occur while you are in bed may accompany hot flashes for menopausal or perimenopausal women. Generally, unless you have a history of heart disease, palpitations are not cause for concern.

YOUR GARDEN TO THE RESCUE

Foods high in magnesium and potassium will help regulate your heartbeat, so add more **potatoes, spinach, nuts,** and **dried beans** to your diet. Grapes and particularly **red grapes** are not only a great source of heart-healthy antioxidants, they are mineral-rich and will give your heart the minerals it needs to function properly.

A few drops of **valerian** tincture can quickly calm a racing heart.

STROKE PREVENTION

YOUR GARDEN RX: watermelon, spinach, broccoli, parsley, tomatoes, brocolli, kale, collards, beets, lettuce

Strokes are often called "brain attacks" because most of them are caused by an obstruction of some sort that cuts off the blood supply to the brain, similar to the way a heart attack occurs when there is an obstruction of coronary blood vessels. However, about 15 percent of strokes are caused by burst blood vessels in the brain.

Atherosclerosis (hardening of the arteries) is a cause of stroke, with the carotid arteries in the neck being the most common place where blood flow is restricted.

The type of stroke caused by burst blood vessels is most often caused by uncontrolled high blood pressure.

YOUR GARDEN TO THE RESCUE

Watermelon and other lycopene-rich foods like **tomatoes** and **papaya** are among the best possible hedges against stroke, since they are well known to protect against heart attacks. If you've had a stroke, opt for lots of raw foods, if you can chew them, or invest in a high-quality juicer to get as many fruits and vegetables into your system as possible.

Foods high in vitamin K, including all the dark green leafy vegetables—**broccoli, kale, collards, spinach**, and **parsley**—will help thin out your blood and lower blood pressure.

Diuretic foods like **beets** and **lettuce** will also help keep your blood pressure under control.

HEMORRHOIDS

YOUR GARDEN RX: apples, dried beans, raspberries, chamomile, comfrey

Hemorrhoids are essentially varicose veins that occur inside your rectum or just around the anus. While they are usually not particularly a threat to your health, they certainly can be annoying with itching, bleeding, and swelling making sitting very uncomfortable.

Constipation and straining to produce a bowel movement cause these veins to rupture, as can pregnancy and labor.

You can prevent hemorrhoids by keeping your bowels healthy and avoiding constipation. If you already have hemorrhoids, preventing constipation is important so they can heal.

YOUR GARDEN TO THE RESCUE

A high-fiber diet is the answer to preventing constipation and preventing irritation of existing hemorrhoids. All fruits and vegetables are good sources of fiber, so eat freely of your garden's bounty.

Pay special attention to getting enough fiber from sources including **apples, dried beans,** and **berries**, like **raspberries.**

A gentle wash of chamomile tea can soothe the pain and itching, as can a salve made from comfrey leaves. (See salve making instructions in Chapter 6.)

HERPES

YOUR GARDEN RX: dried beans, bell peppers, broccoli, strawberries, cantaloupe

The herpes virus manifests in a number of ways, including the chickenpox that many of us experienced in childhood, cold sores, shingles, and the sexually transmitted genital herpes.

After the initial outbreak, the herpes virus remains dormant in your nervous system, sometimes for decades. It is known that people who had chickenpox as children are at risk for painful shingles later in life.

The trigger for shingles and genital herpes outbreaks is not fully understood, but stress is probably a factor in the reawakening of the virus, which then travels up the nerves to the skin, where it multiplies. People with compromised immune systems, such as are found in AIDS patients and those undergoing chemotherapy, are at higher risk for outbreaks.

Those who have genital herpes should never have sex with an uninfected person during an outbreak.

In recent years, a shingles vaccine has become available for people who had chickenpox as children. It has cut the expected outbreaks in half and may reduce the duration and intensity of those that do occur.

YOUR GARDEN TO THE RESCUE

Eating foods rich in the amino acid lysine may shorten outbreaks. You'll find it in abundance in **dried beans**.

It is known that low vitamin C levels can put you at risk for an outbreak. Good sources of vitamin C like **bell peppers, strawberries, broccoli**, and **cantaloupe** will help enhance your immune function and may prevent outbreaks.

HIATAL HERNIA

YOUR GARDEN RX: apples, all types of lettuce, celery, watermelon, cantaloupe, potatoes

A hiatal hernia may produce many of the same symptoms as heartburn, but it is an entirely different problem. This condition occurs when the pyloric valve that separates the esophagus and the stomach becomes stretched, usually because of pregnancy or a large weight gain. It can also be caused by violent coughing, vomiting, or straining with bowel movements. Smokers are at higher risk of hiatal hernia. In some cases, the hernia is present at birth.

The result is that part of the stomach actually pushes up through the diaphragm and into the esophagus.

About 50 percent of Americans over age fifty unknowingly have small hiatal hernias, but they have no symptoms. Large hiatal hernias may cause heartburn, belching, chest pain, and nausea.

Conventional medicine treats hiatal hernia with acid reducers, the same ones used to treat heartburn. Occasionally, surgery is necessary to relieve the pain.

Heavy meals, alcohol, caffeine, smoking, chocolate, citrus fruits, and tomato products tend to aggravate the condition, so most doctors recommend eating several small meals and avoiding trigger foods.

YOUR GARDEN TO THE RESCUE

High-fiber fruits and vegetables, like **apples, lettuce, potatoes** with the skin, and **celery**, will ease the digestive process. You'll also need to drink a lot of water (but not with meals) and eat watery fruits like **watermelon** and **cantaloupe**.

HIVES

YOUR GARDEN RX: chamomile, oregano, comfrey

Hives are itchy swollen patches on your skin that indicate an allergic reaction to something. The trick is figuring out what you're allergic to. It could be a medication, a food, jewelry, pets, insect bites, stress, a type of clothing, or even a soap or laundry detergent.

Generally hives are more annoying than anything else, and, with luck, they fade within a few hours. But sometimes they signal a severe allergic reaction called anaphylaxis, which can be life threatening. If you get hives and have swelling around your mouth or eyes or if you have even the slightest difficulty swallowing, you need to get to an emergency room immediately because the swelling could cut off your ability to breathe.

However, your garden, more specifically your herb garden, can offer some relief for garden variety hives.

YOUR GARDEN TO THE RESCUE

Oregano contains a range of natural anti-allergenics and antihistamines, so a salve or tea made from oregano as well as a few sprigs in your salad or pasta can really help.

Chamomile is the best "go to" herb to calm you down, and a cool wash of chamomile tea will also relieve the itching.

Comfrey salve is a personal favorite of mine, and I use it for any kind of skin irritation.

RX from Outside Your Garden

A paste made of baking soda and water is wonderfully soothing.

HYPERACTIVITY (ATTENTION DEFICIT HYPERACTIVITY DISORDER OR ADHD)

YOUR GARDEN RX: pears, apples, walnuts, pumpkin seeds, dried beans, potatoes, chamomile

ADHD or hyperactivity in children seems to have reached epidemic proportions. The exact causes are unknown, but there has been research that suggests that sugar, chemical additives, and artificial colorings in processed foods may be a cause. Mineral imbalances, particularly an excess amount of copper and insufficient zinc, may also play role in hyperactivity.

Children usually grow out of this disorder by the time they are out of adolescence, but that time lag may seriously impair their education, and consequently, their life prospects.

In the past twenty years or so since ADHD became widely known, parents have learned that restricting simple sugars from their children's diets is usually helpful.

Conventional medicine treats hyperactivity with a variety of anti-anxiety drugs, all of which have potentially serious side effects. Many parents believe that their children are unnecessarily medicated or are overmedicated.

YOUR GARDEN TO THE RESCUE

Zinc-rich foods like **dried beans, pumpkin seeds,** and **potatoes** eaten with the skins on are all helpful in correcting the copper–zinc imbalance that may be a factor in ADHD.

Pears, apples, and other high-fiber foods can slow down the sugar excitability that often accompanies ADHD, but they should be eaten in moderation because they contain substantial amounts of natural sugars themselves.

Walnuts and other high-protein foods are also helpful in slowing the metabolism of simple sugars and potentially easing the hyperactivity symptoms.

HYPOTHYROIDISM

YOUR GARDEN RX: strawberries, asparagus, garlic, spinach, pumpkin seeds, walnuts, pecans

Hypothyroidism means your thyroid gland is not producing enough hormones to properly regulate your metabolism.

Hypothyroidism has a dozen or more symptoms including fatigue, weight gain, dry hair, brittle fingernails, sensitivity to cold, absence of outer third of eyebrows, carpal tunnel syndrome, constipation, and more. Low thyroid function has become increasingly common among perimenopausal women, with an estimated 30 percent or more having low thyroid function by the time they reach menopause.

Hypothyroidism is treated with replacement thyroid hormones. Although natural hormones have been in use for more than fifty years, doctors seem to be more reliant on synthetic thyroid hormone replacement, which can actually increase the symptoms that may have driven you to the doctor in the first place.

Since the thyroid is dependent on iodine to manufacture hormones, insufficient iodine intake can be a factor in the disease.

YOUR GARDEN TO THE RESCUE

Asparagus, strawberries, garlic, and **spinach** are all excellent sources of thyroid-healthy iodine.

Pumpkin seeds are rich in tyrosine, an amino acid that combines with iodine to help your body make thyroid hormones.

Finally, selenium helps convert the plentiful T4 thyroid hormone thyroxine produced by your body into usable T3 (triiodothyronine), the more potent and usable form of thyroid hormones. Find it in abundance in all kinds of nuts, especially the **walnuts** or **pecans** you can grow in many parts of North America.

RX from Outside Your Garden

Celtic sea salt and most fish are excellent sources of iodine.

IMPOTENCE OR LOW LIBIDO

YOUR GARDEN RX: fava beans, garlic, pumpkin seeds, potatoes, turnip greens

Impotence and erectile dysfunction have received lots of attention in recent years because of the popularity of drugs that are supposed to take care of the problem. However, like most pharmaceuticals, the drugs intended to restore sexual function in men carry a price and can even lead to premature death from heart attack in men who were previously healthy.

While impotence was once thought to be mostly a psychological problem, medical science has identified physiological causes in the past couple of decades, most notably in men with diabetes who suffer from impaired circulation and nerve conductivity.

For any man, improving circulation to the small vessels that supply blood to the penis will help, as will improved nerve conductivity to improve sensation.

And yes, there are some men for whom impotence is psychological, so foods that induce relaxation and reduce anxiety can help.

YOUR GARDEN TO THE RESCUE

If you need to relieve sexual anxiety, **fava beans** are among the best foods to help you produce more of the feel-good brain chemical dopamine. Want to really increase the dopamine? Sprout your fava beans to get ten times the dopamine as in plain dried beans.

Garlic helps open blood vessels and improves circulation to all parts of the body, including the small blood vessels that supply the penis.

Zinc-rich **pumpkin seeds** and **potatoes** are good sources of the most important nutrient for sexual function. Those same pumpkin seeds are also good sources of vitamin E to help improve circulation.

Finally, good food sources of B vitamins will help improve nerve function and sensitivity. Fava beans and other dried beans, as well as potatoes, will give you more B.

INDIGESTION

YOUR GARDEN RX: celery, basil, peppermint, rosemary, fennel, chili peppers, radishes

Indigestion is an occasional fact of life for half of all Americans, and for 15 percent of us, it can happen daily. For many chronic sufferers, heartburn is the main symptom, but others experience bloating, belching, gas, nausea, vomiting, stomach rumbling, and diarrhea.

Usually it is caused by simple overeating, a reaction to a particular food to which you may be sensitive, food poisoning, stress, or even a stomach ulcer.

If the indigestion is occasional, it will likely disappear on its own. If it is chronic, you'll need to take a careful look at your food consumption and the amounts you are eating, and pinpoint foods that may be causing a reaction.

YOUR GARDEN TO THE RESCUE

Radishes help calm an old-fashioned stomachache, and **peppermint** tea will soothe that churning feeling and relieve gas and bloating. **Basil**, another member of the mint family, is especially suited to gas relief.

Celery and **rosemary**, both widely prescribed in Europe to treat indigestion, contain dozens of painkillers, anti-inflammatories, anti-ulcer compounds, and sedatives to ease your stomach and intestinal pain.

Chili peppers, contrary to the popular misconception that they trigger bellyaches and heartburn, actually help calm digestion and can even prevent ulcers.

Fennel seeds are a popular tummy soother in India after a satisfying spicy meal.

RX from Outside Your Garden

Ginger is a wonder food that is good for so many things. Its soothing compounds calm an irritated gut, relieve belching and nausea, and help move food through the large and small intestines.

INFECTIONS

YOUR GARDEN RX: garlic, carrots, kale, collards, spinach, strawberries, pumpkin seeds, echinacea

There are numerous types of infections, but all of them stem from a weakened immune system. While it is not possible to avoid infectious bacteria altogether (and we probably shouldn't), a strong immune system will fight off infection and minimize its effect, whether it is from a cut that got dirty or a yeast infection or a viral infection like a cold.

We all know the precautions, especially for colds and flu, but sometimes it is good to give your immune system a challenge that makes it stronger. Not that you should intentionally get an infection, but parents especially seem to be "germophobic" these days. Today's overabundance of antibacterial soaps and hand sanitizers and even countertop cleaners may actually be taking away the body's natural ability to build the immune system.

YOUR GARDEN TO THE RESCUE

Garlic is an excellent source of the natural antibiotic quercetin, which has antiviral, antifungal, and antibacterial benefits. Of course, eating garlic is the best way to boost your immune system whether or not you have an infection. You can also make a garlic poultice to draw out infection from a small wound.

Carrots are a good source of vitamin A to strengthen your immune system and vitamin C to notify it to start an attack against invaders, as are **collards, kale, spinach**, and **strawberries**.

Add in a handful of **pumpkin seeds** for their zinc to boost your production of infection-fighting white blood cells and help you heal quickly.

INFERTILITY

YOUR GARDEN RX: pumpkin seeds, potatoes, dried beans, strawberries
In the modern world with all our stress and rushing from here to there, it's not surprising that infertility has become a problem for many couples.

One on hand, we're exhausted and disinclined to have sex or feel obligated to have it at the right time during the fertile periods. On the other hand, stress, smoking, excessive caffeine and alcohol consumption, and poor diet make our bodies less likely to reproduce, either due to low sperm production in men or irregular ovulation in women.

We're also waiting later and later in life to start our families, and science shows us that both sperm and eggs are less viable as we age.

Recent statistics indicate that at least 10 percent of the couples in America who want to conceive are having difficulty.

Failure to ovulate is the main cause of women's infertility and may be caused by the hormonal fluctuations of perimenopause, which has been identified in many women in their early 30s. Surgeries, miscarriages, infections, and abdominal disease can also cause infertility.

For men, infertility is often caused by erectile dysfunction, which is closely linked to diabetes. Many men also have low sperm production or weak sperm that cannot perform the rigorous task of fertilizing an egg.

A diet that includes lots of antioxidant-rich fruits and vegetables will help both partners.

YOUR GARDEN TO THE RESCUE

For both men and women, eating foods rich in vitamins C, E, and zinc have been shown to be helpful in overcoming infertility. **Strawber ries** and all berries are very good sources of zinc and vitamin C, so they should be a regular part of your diet. Zinc deficiency has been especially identified in low sperm production in men. Low vitamin C levels have been found to slow sperm and cause them clump together.

Potatoes, dried beans, and **pumpkin seeds** are also good sources of zinc and minerals.

RX from Outside Your Garden

If you want to get pregnant, both partners should abstain from smoking, caffeine, and alcohol, since experts say these contribute to infertility problems.

INSECT BITES

YOUR GARDEN RX: comfrey, plantain, pennyroyal

Insect bites have plagued humans and their four-legged friends since the beginning of time. Mosquito and gnat bites are generally annoying, but for the most part, they are not particularly dangerous. Some insect bites, however, can be dangerous, like those of ticks, bees, wasps, fire ants, and certain kinds of spiders.

YOUR GARDEN TO THE RESCUE

Prevention is the best remedy, but avoid toxic commercial bug sprays that contain DEET, which can cause neurological problems and even cardiac arrest.

You can also crush some **pennyroyal** and roll it up in a bandanna to wear around your neck or to tie onto your dog for effective insect repellent.

If you have been bitten, one of the quickest and most effective remedies is to crush or chew a few **plantain** leaves and rub them on the site.

Comfrey is extremely helpful for more serious reactions. I dip a comfrey leaf briefly in boiling water and wrap it around the site, securing it with an old plastic bag or a piece of plastic wrap. The effects of all but the most serious bites will be gone in a few hours. I also make a salve of comfrey and eucalyptus (see Chapter 6) to keep gnats and flies away and heal minor skin problems.

RX from Outside Your Garden

To make a great natural insect repellant, mix five drops of each of the following essential oils in a three-ounce spray bottle of water:

- Eucalyptus
- Pennyroyal
- Citronella
- Lemongrass
- Cedarwood

Apply liberally to yourself and your clothing. It's so effective, I use it on my horses and dogs as well.

INSOMNIA

YOUR GARDEN RX: **sweet corn, dried beans (especially soybeans), Swiss chard, pumpkin seeds, tart cherries, dill, chamomile, valerian, potatoes**

Insomnia affects most of us from time to time, and for about 30 percent of Americans, insomnia is a problem twice or more weekly.

A healthy diet, and especially avoidance of caffeine, are important to getting a good night's sleep, as is good "sleep hygiene," as the experts call it. This means preparing yourself for sleep by gradually winding down your day, avoiding stimulating music or television shows in the evening, perhaps taking a warm bath or drinking a soothing cup of chamomile tea.

One important part of sleep hygiene is to sleep in a room that is as dark as possible. That's because being in the dark prompts your body to produce a hormone called melatonin, the regulator of your waking and sleeping cycles.

YOUR GARDEN TO THE RESCUE

Melatonin-rich foods will help get your sleep cycle back into its natural rhythm. These include **sweet corn** and **tart cherries.**

If your insomnia is due to stress (who hasn't lain awake at night worrying about financial or health issues?), **dill** can help. It's the source of several brain chemicals that ease depression and anxiety, relax muscles, and soothe your nerves.

Nerve-soothing B vitamins, like those found in **dried beans**, can help you sleep. A bonus if you're menopausal: soybeans may give you some hormonal relief.

Tryptophan, those brain chemicals that makes you sleepy after a big Thanksgiving turkey dinner, is a natural asleep inducer. How to grow it in your garden? Try **pumpkin seeds.**

Foods that contain good amounts of magnesium, like **Swiss chard** and **potatoes**, help you sleep because low magnesium can cause your brain to become overstimulated, robbing you of sleep.

Valerian, even though it smells like dirty socks (or worse), is a powerful sleep aid that should be used sparingly. It can have effects similar to those of sleeping pills.

IRRITABLE BOWEL SYNDROME

YOUR GARDEN RX: apples, blueberries, winter squash, spinach, peppermint, fennel, sage, Swiss chard, beet greens
Irritable bowel syndrome is a perplexing and painful basket of symptoms that can range from constipation to diarrhea (often both) and is often characterized by severe gas, bloating, and abdominal cramps.

Since flare-ups can usually be separated into diarrhea-related attacks or constipation-dominant ones, the foods you use to help control IBS will be dependent on which type you are experiencing.

Although the cause of IBS is not entirely understood, it is known that certain things can cause a flare-up, especially such as eating a high-fat meal or simply eating a very large meal.

YOUR GARDEN TO THE RESCUE

If you have the abdominal cramps, bloating, and gas typical of both phases of IBS, it is common sense to avoid dried beans and other gas-producing vegetables like broccoli, cabbage and cucumbers. **Peppermint, fennel**, and **sage**—better yet, all of them together in a tea—are excellent carminatives (anti-gas herbs). Peppermint is also a good stomach soother and relieves cramps.

If you are suffering from a constipation flare-up, look for foods that contain a lot of fiber for a gentle natural laxative effect, like **apples, blueberries, spinach**, and **winter squash**, especially **acorn** and **butternut**. A salad of early spring greens like **spinach, Swiss chard**, and **beet greens** makes an excellent source of fiber and good omega-3 fats to help your bowels get moving.

Apples are a good food for IBS sufferers because they can work both ways, as a natural laxative or to stop diarrhea, bringing your colon back into balance. Look to high-fiber foods to help relieve the diarrhea, too.

JOINT PAIN (ALSO SEE ARTHRITIS)

YOUR GARDEN RX: chili peppers, oregano, spinach, cantaloupe, broccoli, berries

Joint pain is almost always caused by some sort of inflammation of the joints, usually due to wear and tear over the years that causes deterioration of the cartilage, a soft tissue cushion that separates the bones. However, joint pain can be caused by an injury or, in the case of rheumatoid arthritis, by an immune system overreaction to your body's own cartilage.

Over time, joint pain can reduce mobility and negatively affect quality of life.

Inflammatory compounds in highly acidic meats (beef and pork primarily) may aggravate the inflammation, so if you're suffering from joint pain, you might consider cutting back on your red meat intake. For some people, the pain may be caused by an allergic-type reaction to certain kinds of foods. Dairy foods are the most frequent culprits in this type of joint pain, so eliminating them may help. Increasing your water consumption may also help.

Knees, hips, and hands are the most common sites of joint pain, although it can occur anywhere. If you are overweight, losing weight can ease the strain on your joints.

Conventional medical treatment for joint pain is most often NSAIDS (nonsteroidal anti-inflammatory drugs), a class of prescription and non-prescription drugs (like aspirin, acetaminophen, and ibuprofen) that can cause serious problems ranging from gastrointestinal bleeding to heart attacks and liver failure.

YOUR GARDEN TO THE RESCUE:

Capsaicin, a compound found in **chili peppers**, helps reduce pain and inflammation. Eating hot chilies and using a salve or cream made from them (or cayenne pepper) can give you relief. The multifunction beauty of chilies is they also contain salicylates that act like aspirin to relieve pain.

Foods high in vitamin C can help rebuild collagen, the building block of cartilage. Look for your vitamin C in **spinach, cantaloupe, broccoli**, and **berries**.

Oregano is another excellent anti-inflammatory, with dozens of ingredients that help relieve swelling and pain.

RX from Outside Your Garden

Ginger, turmeric, and holy basil (an Indian herb, not the same as our garden basil) have some of the most powerful anti-inflammatory compounds known and they're free of side effects.

KIDNEY STONES

YOUR GARDEN RX: blueberries, radishes, potatoes, cantaloupe, peaches, grapes, dried beans, dandelion

Kidney stones are the result of crystal formation of certain minerals in urine, particularly calcium salts. These minerals actually form tiny rough stones in the kidneys that the body eventually attempts to pass through the ureters (tiny urinary tubes), causing an interruption of urinary flow and intense pain in the lower back, sides, and pelvic area. Kidney stones occur most often in men over fifty. Conventional medicine has, in recent years, developed a nonsurgical shock wave treatment that dissolves larger stones. Increased water intake is key to the treatment of kidney stones to help flush the kidneys and make the urine less acidic.

YOUR GARDEN TO THE RESCUE

Blueberries and **radishes** are well-known diuretics that can help flush the kidneys and help usher out excess mineral deposits. Drinking lots of tea made from **dandelion** leaves and roots can help prevent the formation of kidney stones. **Cantaloupes** and other juicy fruits like **peaches** and **grapes** can help increase your hydration levels. **Potatoes**, high in potassium, can help prevent kidney stones since many sufferers have low potassium levels. **Dried beans**, a good source of magnesium, can help regulate blood calcium and prevent the formation of stones.

RX from Outside Your Garden

Cranberries and cranberry juice are known to be very helpful in addressing and preventing kidney stones and other urinary problems.

LEG PAIN

YOUR GARDEN RX: **garlic, onions, broccoli, cauliflower, tomatoes, sweet potatoes, sunflower seeds, red grapes, dried beans, pumpkin, blueberries, tomatoes**

There are several types of leg pain, ranging from cramps to restless leg syndrome, which can rob you of sleep, to serious conditions like intermittent claudication, a circulatory problem that can be extremely painful and potentially disabling.

YOUR GARDEN TO THE RESCUE

Simple muscle cramps (sometimes we call them charley horses) usually happen when your leg has been in one place for some time and you move it suddenly, causing the muscle to spasm and rebel. Usually the pain subsides in a minute or two with a little stretching and massage. However, if muscle cramps are a common occurrence, you may need more calcium and magnesium in your diet to help your muscles contract and relax properly. **Broccoli, tomatoes** (better yet, tomato juice), **sweet potatoes**, and **sunflower seeds** are good sources of essential magnesium and potassium that will help prevent leg cramps.

Iron deficiency is a contributor to restless leg syndrome, so if you've experienced that can't-sit-or-lie-still feeling, look at your iron intake and see if it is lacking. While red meat is the best source of iron, you can get moderate amounts in **dried beans**, especially **kidney beans** and **pumpkin.**

Intermittent claudication with severe cramping and tingling in thighs, buttocks, and legs is a form of peripheral artery disease (PAD) that can be serious. It is caused by clogged blood vessels in the legs and puts you at risk of a heart attack. People with PAD often experience great pain even when they try walking a short distance. Because PAD is a heart disease, following the guidelines for cholesterol, blood pressure, and other heart-related problems is helpful.

Red grapes and **blueberries** are among the most powerful antioxidants and will promote heart health. **Garlic** and **onions** are also antioxidants with special properties that make blood less likely to clot.

LIVER DISEASE

YOUR GARDEN RX: apples, onions, green beans, grapes, broccoli, dried beans, spinach, milk thistle, celery

Liver disease is a serious problem that can have a variety of causes, primarily including hepatitis B (liver cancer), alcoholism (cirrhosis), and obesity (fatty liver disease). Since the liver is the organ that cleanses the body of toxins, stores fat-soluble vitamins, and manufactures amino acids and cholesterol, any disease that affects the liver has far-ranging and serious consequences.

However, the liver has a unique ability among the body's organs: It can function even if only 25 percent of it is healthy enough and the damaged cells can be regenerated.

YOUR GARDEN TO THE RESCUE

Flavonoids, nature's warrior antioxidants, can be particularly helpful in fighting liver disease. In European countries, silymarin, a particular flavonoid found in **milk thistle**, actually saved the lives of many people with cirrhosis.

Other flavonoid-rich foods that promote liver health include **onions, green beans, grapes, broccoli, celery**, and **spinach**.

Dried beans and **leafy greens** are also good sources of omega-3 fatty acids that promote good liver function, and the dried beans are also good sources of protein.

LUPUS

YOUR GARDEN RX: broccoli, cabbage, pumpkin seeds, sunflower seeds, borage

Systemic lupus erythematosus, commonly called lupus, is an autoimmune disease that has many arthritis-like symptoms, including severe joint pain.

Its cause is unknown, although there is speculation that lupus may be caused by a virus. For many people, lupus is a manageable disease, but in severe cases, it can cause organ failure, usually starting with the kidneys. In those cases, it is life threatening.

Among the many symptoms of lupus is extreme sensitivity to sunlight, so many people with the disease are deficient in vitamin D, a hormone-like vitamin that the body manufactures through exposure to sunlight.

Since people with lupus tend to have high cholesterol levels, you might want to look at the Heart Disease entry in this chapter.

Some foods may increase the intensity of the symptoms of lupus. It's usually best to avoid foods that have alfalfa in any form. Also, for many people, mushrooms and some smoked foods may cause problems.

Lupus is often treated with NSAIDS (nonsteroidal anti-inflammatory drugs), but in severe cases, steroids are necessary to control the pain. While there is no cure for this potentially deadly disease, lifestyle and medical management can often control it.

YOUR GARDEN TO THE RESCUE

Flavonoid-rich cruciferous vegetables like **broccoli** and **cabbage** contain substances called indoles that are helpful in cleansing the body of harmful types of estrogen, a concern since most lupus sufferers are women.

Pumpkin and **sunflower seeds** are good sources of vitamin E, zinc, and selenium, all important to people with lupus to help them fight inflammation.

Borage and evening primrose are important sources of gamma-linolenic acid (GLA), unique fatty acids that balance the acidic and inflammatory acids we encounter when we eat meat.

MENOPAUSE AND PERIMENOPAUSE

YOUR GARDEN RX: black beans, dried beans, celery, dill, fennel, walnuts

Hormone fluctuations begin long before a woman stops menstruating. Some women start experiencing perimenopause, which is when estrogen and progesterone start leapfrogging, as early as their mid-thirties.

When a woman enters menopause it means she no longer has menstrual periods (medically defined as having no periods for 12 months) and is no longer able to become pregnant. Postmenopausal women have a greater risk of heart attack and stroke because they have lost the protective effects of estrogen. Bones may also become more brittle at this stage of life, necessitating mineral supplementation to prevent osteoporosis.

Perimenopause carries with it a laundry list of unpleasant symptoms, including hot flashes, night sweats, mood swings, depression, memory loss, joint pain, and weight gain.

YOUR GARDEN TO THE RESCUE

Black beans and other **dried beans** are a good source of plant estrogens (saponins, phytosterols, isoflavones, and lignans) without some of the potential estrogenic excesses of soy, and they may actually help protect you against estrogen-related cancers like breast cancer.

Celery, dill, and **fennel**, all of which are in the same plant family, have mild and gentle estrogenic compounds to relieve symptoms like hot flashes and give you long-term protection against heart disease and cancer.

RX from Outside Your Garden

The soy controversy: Some experts think soy will naturally help replace lost estrogen, and others think it is harmful. There's not much doubt that soy will relieve hot flashes, but there are other less risky means of addressing this symptom such as supplements made from black cohosh, chasteberry, or wild yam.

Walnuts are an excellent source of omega-3 fatty acids that can help preserve memory, lessen mood swings, and ease depression and hot flashes.

When perimenopause is over and you are officially menopausal or postmenopausal, you'll want to follow all the guidelines to protect your heart and bones and prevent cancer. You may continue to experience some of the symptoms of menopause for several years. A diet rich in all kinds of garden goodies will help keep you healthy for years to come.

MENSTRUAL DISORDERS AND PMS

YOUR GARDEN RX: **dried beans, walnuts, sweet potatoes, apples, carrots, tomatoes, strawberries, cantaloupe, parsley, brocoli, kale, spinach, pumpkin seeds**

Menstrual "inconveniences" are common. Most women experience some problems, either before their periods or during them: cramping, breast tenderness, constipation or diarrhea, mood swings, irritability, bloating, headaches, and food cravings. This is generally known as PMS (premenstrual syndrome). Its basket of symptoms can be a minor annoyance or a major life challenge, depending on its severity.

Research shows that women who exercise several times a week are less likely to have PMS. PMS is also less prevalent in women who engage in healthy eating habits, avoiding processed foods, caffeine, and alcohol in the days leading up to their periods.

Conventional medicine doesn't have much to offer women who suffer from severe menstrual problems except NSAIDS like ibuprofen, which may be moderately effective, and antidepressants, which aren't very effective in their own right.

YOUR GARDEN TO THE RESCUE

B vitamins go a long way toward soothing jangled nerves, so increase your intake of B-rich **dried beans** and **sweet potatoes** in the days before your period begins to keep your mood on a more even keel.

Walnuts are a great source of magnesium to ease mood swings and cramping, plus they are a good source of pain- and inflammation-relieving omega-3 fatty acids. **Broccoli, kale**, and other cruciferous vegetables are also helpful against cramps because of their muscle-relaxing calcium content.

Even a tablespoon or two of fresh **parsley** will help ease bloating, and fiber-dense, moderately sweet **apples** and **carrots** can quell the sugar cravings if you give them twenty minutes or so to take effect.

If you have unusually heavy periods, you are at risk for anemia, so increasing your iron intake is a good idea. Since you don't want to "beef up" too much with red meat (which remains the best source of iron), look for iron-rich veggies like **spinach** (remember Popeye the Sailor Man?), **pumpkin seeds**, and **dried beans**. **Tomatoes, strawberries, cantaloupe**, and other good sources of vitamin C will help you absorb the iron better.

MUSCLE CRAMPS

YOUR GARDEN RX: spinach, collards, potatoes, dried beans, sweet potatoes, beet greens, tomatoes

Muscle cramps are caused by a muscle that contracts and then doesn't relax or goes into a spasm, contracting and relaxing rapidly. If you've ever felt the pain of a charley horse, you don't forget it soon.

While calf muscles most often suffer charley horses, any muscles can cramp. It's common to have cramps in feet, hands, and back muscles.

Muscle cramps are more common in hot weather and, since dehydration is one cause of muscle cramping, inadequate water intake in the summer probably contributes to the cramping.

Muscles can't move unless they receive a message from the brain, and minerals are the carriers of those messages. If you have a shortfall of any of the electrolyte minerals—calcium, potassium, sodium, or magnesium—your muscles are more likely to cramp. While all these minerals are important to muscle contraction, magnesium is the controller, and a shortfall of magnesium can keep the others from being absorbed.

YOUR GARDEN TO THE RESCUE

Clearly, magnesium-rich foods like **potatoes** with the skins on, and **dried beans**, especially black-eyed peas and kidney and pinto beans, are a big part of the answer to muscle cramps.

Potatoes are a great bet here, because they are also an excellent source of cramp-relieving potassium, as are **sweet potatoes, beet greens**, and **tomatoes.**

Leafy greens, including **spinach** and **collards**, are good sources of potassium as well, and they are also rich in calcium for added relief from involuntary muscle contractions.

NAIL PROBLEMS

YOUR GARDEN RX: dried beans, broccoli, peas, spinach, raspberries, cantaloupe, tomatoes, celery, garlic, chamomile

Nails are a barometer of your overall health. Although you may sometimes nervously pick at your fingernails or bite them, brittle, breaking, and thin nails are most often indicators of a nutrient deficiency. They also can be a symptom of certain types of anemia or hypothyroidism. (See the entries about these conditions for more information.) In addition, some nail problems are caused by fungal infections.

To be strong, your nails need a steady supply of high-quality protein. Like every other part of your body, they are also dependent on adequate water to remain moist.

Weak and brittle nails can also be caused by our affection for manicures and pedicures. The harsh chemicals in polish removers and the formaldehyde in many nail polishes can damage nails. Artificial nails can cause severe damage to the nails and further weaken them by making them susceptible to fungal infection.

YOUR GARDEN TO THE RESCUE

Dried beans are among the best vegetable sources of iron, so include some in your diet daily if you want to improve your nail health. **Broccoli, peas**, and **spinach** are also good sources of iron.

You'll want to add foods high in vitamin C to help your body absorb the iron: **raspberries, cantaloupe**, and **tomatoes**.

If your problems are caused by a fungal infection, eating celery and garlic can help your system fight off the infection. If you are bold enough, you can also make a poultice of mashed **garlic** or a wash of **chamomile** tea, since chamomile has more than two dozen antiseptic compounds.

NAUSEA

YOUR GARDEN RX: peppermint, sage, fennel, cilantro, rosemary, oreg-ano, potatoes, chamomile, raspberry

Nausea can have a number of causes, ranging from simple indigestion to pregnancy-related morning sickness, motion sickness, headaches, and even food poisoning.

Most people have no interest whatever in eating when they are nause-ated, although in some cases, dry toast or a little rice may help calm the queasies. Sometimes the easiest way is to go ahead and vomit and get it over with, even if you have an aversion to the loss of control that accom-panies vomiting.

Be sure to drink as much water as you can comfortably get down when you're feeling queasy to avoid dehydration, but it is absolutely fine to skip eating for a day or even two unless you have diabetes. Water intake is especially important if you have a tummy bug that is also giving you diarrhea.

YOUR GARDEN TO THE RESCUE

If you feel at all like eating, go with something very mild and bland, like a plain baked **potato.** While some people think dairy foods are a good idea, milk or cottage cheese can actually worsen the problem if you're queasy.

Turn to your herb garden for the best answers and the quickest relief. Concoct a tea containing as many of the following herbs as you like:

- **Peppermint**, for general digestive calming
- **Oregano**, for its sedative and pain-relieving properties
- **Cilantro** (or **coriander**) and **chamomile**, which can actually help you vomit if that is what you need
- **Fennel**, famous in India for its indigestion relief
- **Raspberry** leaf, which is so safe it is widely recommended for morning sickness
- **Sage** and **rosemary**, for their stomach-calming properties as well as helping to ease the anxiety that often accompanies nausea

NERVE PAIN

YOUR GARDEN RX: spinach, potatoes, melon, sunflower seeds, pumpkin seeds

Nerve pain can have a number of causes:

1. An accident may have damaged or constricted nerves, causing them to either send unceasing pain signals or to become numb.
2. Shingles and other herpes outbreaks are caused by the herpes virus, often acquired if you had chickenpox as a child, which remains dormant in the nervous system until a flare-up through the nerves occurs, often decades later.
3. Sciatica is a type of nerve pain primarily caused by degenerating discs in the lower back.
4. Diabetes can cause peripheral neuropathy, a numbing of the nerves usually in the feet, that leads to more amputations than any other non–accident-related cause.
5. Many medications, including those used for chemotherapy, can cause nerve damage.
6. Nutritional deficiencies, most often of vitamin B12, can cause weakness or burning sensations.
7. There are also a number of diseases, like Lou Gehrig's disease (amyotrophic lateral sclerosis) and trigeminal neuralgia, that affect the nerves.

YOUR GARDEN TO THE RESCUE

Nerves are directly affected by B-complex vitamins, so look for B-rich foods like **spinach, potatoes**, and **melons** to help ease nerve pain. Note: One of the best nerve-pain relievers is vitamin B12, found only in animal products.

Vitamin E shortfalls can also cause a form of neuralgia, so be sure you're getting enough E with **sunflower** and **pumpkin seeds**.

YOUR GARDEN RX: potatoes, turnips, rutabagas, apples, dried beans, grapes, chili peppers

If you've been trying to control your weight, you know very well that it's an incredibly complex task. Doctors and other so-called experts (they're not!) will tell you that you need to eat less and exercise more. They'll also tell you that it is "calories in/calories burned"—a mathematical equation. It's not that simple.

Each individual's biological makeup is unique. That's why your best friend (especially if he's male) can annoyingly skip lunch and lose five pounds while you eat like a bird for weeks and the scale doesn't budge a bit. Your weight depends on a broad spectrum of variables, including your body type, metabolic rate, heredity, amount of body fat, and, of course, caloric intake. Yes, calories do play a part—but they are not the whole story.

I wish I could give you more encouragement, but the best advice is to get to know your own body. It's surprising how many of us do not. The basics are no-brainers:

- Eat when you're hungry.
- Stop eating when you are full.
- Don't eat when you're not hungry.
- Especially don't eat when you are stressed.
- Avoid multitasking when you eat to prevent overeating.
- Chew your food carefully.
- Drink lots of water, but not with meals.
- And perhaps most important, enjoy your food!

YOUR GARDEN TO THE RESCUE

You can freely eat virtually all fruits and vegetables when you are trying to control your weight. You may be surprised to learn that includes **potatoes**, an underrated vegetable with a multitude of health benefits. Among them, potatoes help you feel full longer, helping you avoid the temptations of less healthful foods. Other starchy root vegetable like **turnips** and **rutabagas** have the same effect. Of course, as always, it's best to forgo the butter and sour cream. Salsa makes a healthy diet-friendly topping for baked potatoes.

Apples are another "high satisfaction" food, low on the glycemic index, low in calories, and full of appetite-satisfying fiber and pectin.

All **dried beans** are high in fiber, low in fat, low in calories, and packed with health benefits, so they're among the best foods you can adopt for weight control.

The same goes for all kinds of **hot peppers**: they're nutrient dense, low in calories, nonexistent on the fat scale, and their "heat" helps rev up your metabolism. Try adding a little hot sauce to that salsa on your baked potato.

OSTEOPOROSIS

YOUR GARDEN RX: blackberries, broccoli, cauliflower, dried beans, kale, cabbage, collards

Osteoporosis is a loss of bone density over time, usually affecting the elderly and most often postmenopausal women. The first sign of osteoporosis is usually a loss of height due to the weakening of the spine due to bone loss. Bone pain, tenderness, fractures with little or no trauma, and back and neck pain due to fractures of spinal bones are common.

The primary cause of osteoporosis is low estrogen levels in women after menopause. It can also be caused by smoking, excessive alcohol consumption, rheumatoid arthritis, chronic kidney disease, hyperparathyroidism, eating disorders, and the long-term use of corticosteroid medications like prednisone and methylprednisolone.

Conventional medicine mainly treats osteoporosis with a class of drugs called bisphosphonates, which attach themselves to calcium molecules in the bones and slow the breakdown of bone tissue. The biggest concern with these drugs has been that they can actually cause fractures that are exceptionally difficult to treat and they've specifically been associated with deterioration of the jawbone.

YOUR GARDEN TO THE RESCUE

Food rich in calcium may help strengthen your bones. Better yet, opt for garden produce that gives you a wide variety of minerals essential to bone health, including magnesium, manganese, copper, phosphorous, and potassium. **Blackberries** are excellent sources of many different minerals, so add them to your diet on a daily basis, if possible. **Broccoli, cauliflower, kale, cabbage**, and **collards** are also not only good sources of calcium, they are also mineral dense.

Dried beans are among our best vegetable sources of protein, an important building block for strengthening bones and important to the production of hormones that help build bone tissue.

PAIN RELIEF

YOUR GARDEN RX: chili peppers, oregano, peppermint

Pain is a very subjective thing that can come from many sources and have many causes. Even though none of us like pain, it actually is your friend and lets you know when something is wrong. Imagine the consequences if you didn't feel pain when you put your hand on a hot stove.

Pain signals are carried along nerve pathways to the brain. The brain interprets the pain and takes action, if necessary, such as pulling your hand back from the hot stove or putting your hand on your jaw if you have a toothache.

But we all know that pain can be much more than a minor inconvenience. It can disrupt our lives, whether it's a simple toothache or something really serious. Chronic pain can certainly have life-altering effects.

Conventional medicine treats long-term pain with increasingly addictive painkillers and sometimes antidepressants and antianxiety drugs as well.

YOUR GARDEN TO THE RESCUE

Capsaicin, the primary ingredient in **hot peppers**, is one of nature's most powerful pain relievers precisely because it blocks those pain signals to the brain using "Substance P," a pain-relieving element of capsaicin that science hasn't yet entirely defined. But science does know that it works for pain signals that travel along the nerves. It won't work for the pain of a strained muscle.

You can make a capsaicin cream by adding finely chopped chilies to your favorite hand cream. When you apply it, your skin must be completely dry or you'll get a burning sensation that will be its own pain.

You also can chop the chilies into a soup, stew, or salad or just add a few drops of hot sauce to your favorite foods.

Oregano is a literal soup of painkillers, as is **peppermint**, so drinking them as a tea or making a salve from them can give you relief.

RX from Outside Your Garden

Ginger is one of the most potent anti-inflammatories known, so a tea or even a ginger salve can relieve pain effectively. With its dozens of healing ingredients, it's a good idea to keep ginger on hand at all times.

PNEUMONIA

YOUR GARDEN RX: blueberry, spinach, sweet potatoes, garlic, elderberry, onion, celery, oregano, rosemary, basil

Pneumonia is most often the result of a challenged immune system. That means it rarely occurs by itself but comes in the aftermath of an immune system challenge like a cold, flu, bronchitis, or a hospital-acquired infection.

Pneumonia can be life threatening and is tricky to treat because it can be caused by a virus or by bacteria, with the added complication that many modern pneumonia strains are antibiotic resistant. Infrequently pneumonia can be caused by a fungal infection.

Conventional medicine usually treats pneumonia with antibiotics, which will be ineffective if the cause is viral or fungal and only moderately effective if it is bacterial.

YOUR GARDEN TO THE RESCUE

Prevention is your best defense against pneumonia, so any vegetables, fruit, or herbs that boost your immune system will serve you well. These include antioxidant-rich **blueberries, sweet potatoes, spinach**, and citrus fruits if you can grow them. Preventing colds and flu or treating them at the outset is the second prong in our approach to pneumonia prevention. **Garlic** is a star here again because of its antimicrobial properties, meaning it can fight viral, bacterial, and fungal infections. **Onions, elderberries, celery, oregano, rosemary**, and **basil** also carry those antimicrobial properties. A general diet rich in these foods will help prevent colds and flu, and increasing your intake at the first sign of these illnesses will help prevent pneumonia.

ROSACEA

YOUR GARDEN RX: cherries, blackberries, blueberries, comfrey

Rosacea is a skin condition similar to acne, without the characteristic blackheads you'd find with acne.

Most information about rosacea and food contains warnings to avoid hot, spicy foods that increase blood flow to the face. Many sources also recommend limiting alcohol, sugar, caffeine, and animal fats. Not coincidentally, most of these rosacea triggers are acidic foods, and there is a school of thought that alkalinizing your diet will also help relieve the condition.

YOUR GARDEN TO THE RESCUE

Cherries, blackberries, and **blueberries** help constrict swollen and inflamed blood vessels, including those tiny ones that make your face red.

Comfrey, used as a salve or cream, can also help constrict those inflamed blood vessels and reduce redness. It is not advisable to use comfrey as a tea because there are some reports it can be toxic to the liver.

SINUSITIS

YOUR GARDEN RX: chili peppers, bell peppers, garlic, onions, oregano
Sinusitis is an infection in the sinuses, those hollow cavities around your face to which we rarely pay attention until they fill up with mucus and cause pressure, headaches, postnasal drip, cough, and general misery.

Sinusitis generally follows a cold and can be caused by viruses, bacteria, fungi, or all three. Usually the infection clears up on its own in four to six weeks, but those weeks can feel very long indeed with the misery of sinusitis.

Sinusitis can also be triggected by allergies, most often to cigarette smoke, but some food allergies can also trigger the immune reaction.

Conventional medicine usually treats sinusitis with antibiotics, which may be effective if the infection is bacterial but will be completely ineffective if it is viral or fungal. Nasal sprays are also often used, but these can become habit forming.

YOUR GARDEN TO THE RESCUE

The congestion is caused by the formation of histamines, chemical compounds your body produces when you're having an allergic reaction. **Garlic** and **onions** are the best sources of quercetin, a compound that acts like an antihistamine and also helps reduce inflammation.

Bell peppers and other food sources of vitamin C boost your immune system and offer the added benefit of natural defense against viral infections.

Oregano is an excellent natural antihistamine and offers bonus antiseptic and antioxidant benefits, so think about a vitamin C–rich **tomato** sauce heavily spiced with oregano when you have sinus problems.

RX from Outside Your Garden

Washing your sinuses with warm, filtered saltwater is one of the best ways to treat sinusitis and to prevent its return. Use sea salt to prevent irritation, and either slowly "drink" the water through your nose from a glass, spitting it out your mouth, or use one of those handy neti pots designed just for this purpose.

SMOKING CESSATION

YOUR GARDEN RX: apples, celery, broccoli, strawberries, cherries, tomatoes, pumpkin

If you're a smoker, you've heard it over and over again: You *must* stop before you do irreparable damage to your health. Some say it is more difficult to stop smoking than to beat a heroin addiction, so use whatever tools you have, even prescription drugs, to overcome this deadly addiction. Ask your doctor for help.

Yes, it will be difficult, but it is also the most positive thing you can do for yourself and those you love. Having a buddy along the way will help, as will participating in one of the many support groups in every city and town.

Many people who smoke are worried that they will gain weight when they quit and it's true, there is an association between stopping smoking and gaining weight. Look for foods that help stop cravings—not only for cigarettes, but for food.

YOUR GARDEN TO THE RESCUE

Look for foods known to help stop cravings, primarily **apples** and **celery**, both of which contain anti-craving substances.

According to an interesting study from Duke University, smokers reported that eating fruits and vegetables made their cigarettes taste worse. That may be why smokers eat far fewer fruits and vegetables than do nonsmokers.

You'll also want to increase your intake of foods that protect you from the free-radical damage associated with cigarette smoking. **Broccoli** and other cruciferous vegetables are among the best at this, providing several excellent anticancer compounds, including sulphoraphane.

Cherries and **strawberries** contain a unique phytochemical, ellagic acid, which neutralizes hydrocarbons, especially the cancer-causing chemicals in tobacco smoke.

Tomatoes and other pink- and red-colored fruits offer antioxidant protection through a carotenoid called lycopene, which has been shown to offer more cancer protection than most other fruits and vegetables.

Pumpkin and other orange or yellow veggies and fruits may protect against cancers most commonly attributed to smokers—lung, colon, skin, and kidney—because of their high levels of beta carotene.

RX from Outside Your Garden

Stop cravings with the amino acid l-glutamine. Just break open a capsule and sprinkle its tasteless contents on your tongue. L-glutamine can banish even the strongest cravings for cigarettes and is even effective for drug addictions.

SPRAINS

YOUR GARDEN RX: cabbage, parsley, calendula, arnica

A bad sprain can sometimes take longer to heal than a broken bone because the injury to soft tissue, ligaments, and muscles can be slow to heal.

Sprains involve stretching or tearing of the ligaments and muscles. The most common sprain site is the ankle. If the ligament is ruptured (you may hear a loud popping sounds when this occurs), surgery may be necessary.

Conventional medicine also wisely recommends keeping the inflamed area cool with ice, elevating it to the level of the heart, and avoiding using the affected area as much as possible.

YOUR GARDEN TO THE RESCUE

The advice of conventional medicine is sound, but you may be able to speed the healing with a poultice made of **cabbage** leaves or **parsley**, both folk remedies that help reduce swelling and ease the pain. Parsley has the added benefit of increasing circulation in the injured area and speeding healing.

Calendula (a marigold-like flower easily grown in most North American gardens) and **arnica** (a daisylike flower found mostly in the western states) both have anti-inflammatory properties and are best used in a salve or cream.

STRESS

YOUR GARDEN RX: potatoes, celery, green beans, borage, lavender, chamomile

It's impossible to avoid stress in this modern world. From the moment we get up in the morning, whether we flip on the radio for the morning news or wrangle kids into their school clothes while preparing lunches and getting dressed for work, for most of us the day begins with stress-inducing situations and ends the same way as, exhausted, we fall into bed at night. Often the stress doesn't even end at bedtime as we toss and turn, unable to sleep because of the to-do lists running through our minds, then waken the next morning short on sleep to start the stress cycle all over again.

When we are stressed, our adrenal glands release a hormone called cortisol, which was utilized by our ancient fight-or-flight mechanism to help us escape from saber-toothed tigers. Cortisol gives us that quick burst of energy, the pounding heart, the superhuman strength, and heightened reflexes. But in our modern world, those saber-toothed tigers never go away and we experience chronically elevated cortisol, with a host of negative effects: high blood sugar, increased amounts of dangerous abdominal fat, high blood pressure, reduced immunity, impaired memory, and the health conditions that result from these conditions.

It is estimated that 90 percent of all visits to the doctor's office are stress related—not illnesses that are "all in your head" or hypochondria—and we know there is a stress component to many diseases.

There are many ways to manage stress, ranging from meditation and yoga to exercise and socializing. There are also caveats: get enough sleep, and avoid cigarettes and overuse of alcohol and caffeine.

YOUR GARDEN TO THE RESCUE

There are also many food-based ways to address your stress and move into the "cool zone."

Potatoes and other starchy vegetables are good stress relievers, largely because our culture views them as comfort foods. That's because carbohydrates can actually cause changes to brain chemistry that raise levels of the feel-good brain chemical serotonin, making you feel more relaxed.

Celery can also help relieve stress-related hypertension because it relaxes muscles, including the arterial muscles that we tense up in stressful times.

The high levels of B vitamins as well as vitamins A and C in **green beans** affect the nervous system and help bring about a sense of calm when you are feeling jittery.

From your herb garden, **lavender** (a sprinkle of flowers in your bath water), **borage** (as a tea), and **chamomile** in any form are the quintessential stress relievers. They should be staples in your herb collection.

SUNBURN

YOUR GARDEN RX: cucumbers, eggplant, potato, tomato, chamomile

We've all been there, intentionally or not: We've been too long in the sun and find ourselves with a painful burn. When it happens only occasionally, it's a minor inconvenience. The sunburn will usually fade within days (and you most likely won't be tan underneath). You may need to avoid the friends who invariably want to slap you on the back during this time, and the outer layer of skin may peel, but in the short term, sunburn is no big deal.

In the long term, however, repeated sunburns can be a very big deal, significantly increasing your risk of skin cancers, including potentially deadly melanoma.

When you're out in the sun, wear a hat. Better yet, if you're out for more than a few minutes, put on a zinc oxide–based sunscreen, the safest kind around.

YOUR GARDEN TO THE RESCUE

A cool **cucumber** paste will ease the pain quickly, as will pulverized **eggplant**.

Rubbing a cut **potato** on the burned area will ease the pain, as will a cool **chamomile** tea wash.

If you're looking for a natural sunscreen, add **tomatoes** to your diet on a regular basis. The lycopene in tomatoes gives you natural sun protection from within, but don't count on that for complete sun protection. You'll still need sunscreen (a natural one!), hat, and protective clothing.

TOOTHACHE

YOUR GARDEN RX: chili peppers, oregano

Most of us get a little tooth pain from time to time—maybe from eating ice (a bad habit I have been unable to break) or tooth sensitivity to heat or cold. Tooth pain in adults, if it continues for more than a couple of days, requires dental care because it could signal a cavity, a cracked tooth, an abscess, or other infection. It can even signal something serious and non–dental related; for example, it can be an uncommon signal for angina chest pain that can be a signal of heart disease.

Tooth pain in children is familiar because it signals tooth-fairy time. There is no need for dental intervention unless the tooth doesn't come out on its own.

RX from Outside Your Garden

My grandmother always kept a bottle of clove oil in her medicine cabinet, and I have fond memories of her dabbing it on my gums when my baby teeth were falling out and adult teeth coming in. The pain would vanish almost immediately.

YOUR GARDEN TO THE RESCUE

Okay, go ahead and cringe, but a cut **hot pepper**, which will initially burn when applied to the painful area, will soon cancel out the pain signals.

The pain relief will probably last two to three hours, when you can repeat the process. Hot peppers also contain salicylates—painkillers similar to aspirin.

Not yet ready to go the chili-pepper route? Try **oregano**. Make a strong tea and swish it around in your mouth for pain relief and ammunition against infection if that is what is causing the pain.

TOXIN OVERLOAD

YOUR GARDEN RX: beets, blueberries, bok choy, broccoli, carrots, sweet potatoes, onions, apples, strawberries, watermelon, bell peppers, milk thistle, red clover

All of us are exposed to a soup of toxins every day. Even if you are lucky enough to be able to eat a totally organic diet, you're still being bombarded by toxins all around you, ranging from polluted air to household and industrial chemicals, cosmetics and personal care products, pollutants in municipal water, cigarette smoke, and offgassing carpets and furniture in our own homes or in places we visit.

It is virtually impossible to avoid exposure to these toxins, but it is certainly possible to help sweep them from our systems. Since the liver is the body's primary organ of detoxification (we also detoxify through the breathing process and through our urine and sweat), look for foods that help support optimal liver function to help detoxify your body.

YOUR GARDEN TO THE RESCUE

Beets help purify your blood and cleanse your liver with the help of a unique blend of phytochemicals.

Blueberries have a rare ability to stop toxins from crossing the blood–brain barrier and entering the fatty tissues of the brain.

Cruciferous vegetables like **bok choy, broccoli**, and more contain in their health arsenal the ability to neutralize some of the pollutants in cigarette smoke and also stimulate the liver to produce the enzyme it needs for detoxification.

Beta carotene, like that found in **carrots** and **sweet potatoes**, helps sweep heavy metals out of the body. The pectin in **apples** binds to the heavy metals and helps neutralize them so they can be safely eliminated from the body.

Onions, one of our superfoods, has been shown to help thin the blood, and they also cleanse it and help detoxify the respiratory tract.

Vitamin C–rich foods, like **strawberries, watermelon,** and **bell peppers**, help the body produce glutathione, which supports healthy liver function and helps neutralize damage from environmental toxins.

Milk thistle has traditionally been used to protect the liver from damage from toxins, and it can also protect from damage from certain drugs, such as acetaminophen (most commonly known as Tylenol), that can cause liver damage. Milk thistle may actually help the liver grow new cells and repair itself.

Finally, **red clover** helps the body rid itself of excess mucus and fluids. It's often prescribed by herbalists (flowers and leaves dried and used as a tea) to enhance the cleansing action of liver, kidneys, and the lymphatic system.

VAGINITIS/YEAST INFECTIONS

YOUR GARDEN RX: blackberry, garlic, spinach, dried beans, oregano, chamomile, calendula

Most vaginal infections are caused by yeast overgrowth in the vagina. There is much speculation about the cause of these types of fungal infections, but it almost certainly due to dysbiosis, an imbalance of friendly and unfriendly microorganisms in the digestive tract. When the imbalance becomes extreme, *Candida albicans* yeast, which is naturally present in the digestive tract, can begin to grow out of control, eventually permeating the intestinal walls and lodging in any of a number of places in the body, including the vagina.

If you've taken antibiotics recently, that has likely contributed to the imbalance, as do taking birth control pills and excess sugar consumption (yeast literally loves to "eat" sugar). Conventional medicine sometimes treats vaginitis with antibiotics, which are useless against fungal infections.

YOUR GARDEN TO THE RESCUE

We have an arsenal of foods and herbs that can help rein in that yeast overgrowth. **Garlic**, with its abundance of sulfur compounds, is a natural antifungal, as is **oregano**.

Blackberries, spinach, and **dried beans** are good sources of the B vitamin folic acid, which may help protect you from vaginal infections.

Calendula is a natural astringent with the ability to help your body fight off all types of infections, including fungal infections. Calendula is most commonly made into a salve.

A **chamomile** tea or wash or flowers added to your bath water can ease the pain and itching associated with vaginitis.

VARICOSE VEINS

YOUR GARDEN RX: blueberries, grapes, parsley, bay leaves, cabbage
Varicose veins are ropy, enlarged veins (spider veins are smaller versions), usually in the legs, cosmetically inelegant, but most often no more than a nuisance, although sometimes they are the source of a dull ache or pain and swelling. However, varicose veins can increase your risk for more serious circulatory problems. Conventional medicine recommends compression stocking to help assist the veins in returning blood to the heart. In serious cases, various types of surgery may be considered.

YOUR GARDEN TO THE RESCUE

Virtually all fruits and vegetables have some levels of antioxidants called flavonoids. Flavonoids like those found in **grapes** can reduce the permeability of blood vessels so the stronger blood vessels don't leak blood and fluids into the surrounding tissue. A particular flavonoid compound called rutin has been study-proven to help strengthen capillaries and improve varicose veins. You'll find rutin in **parsley, blueberries**, citrus fruits, and buckwheat. **Blueberries** and **grapes** are extra helpful because they are also good sources of capillary-strengthening anthocyanins. Poultices made of bay leaves and/or cabbage warmed in olive oil have long been used as a topical remedy to reduce varicose veins and relieve swelling.

WARTS

YOUR GARDEN RX: garlic, onion, spinach, dried beans, potatoes
As many as 10 percent of us get these unsightly growths, which most frequently occur on hands, feet, and genitals. While there is no validation for the old wives' tale that toads cause warts, it is known that they are caused by the human papillomavirus (HPV) and they can be contagious, particularly if you are immune-compromised and you have contact with someone with genital warts.

YOUR GARDEN TO THE RESCUE

Simply rubbing a clove of **garlic** or a sliced **onion** on an external wart can give you enough antimicrobial sulfur compounds to knock out the virus that causes warts. Some people prefer to take their garlic infused in oil or even internally. You wouldn't want to put garlic directly on genital warts or on a baby's skin, because it could be strong enough to burn. Eating **spinach, potatoes, dried beans**, and other zinc-rich foods is known to help boost immune function and even specifically to help get rid of warts.

PART 2

HOW TO GROW YOUR HEALING FOODS

A garden always gives back more than it receives.

—Mara Beamish

CHAPTER 3

Gardening Basics

Here's the good news: Anyone can garden, regardless of the space you have available. I remember fondly my friend Meg's minuscule Manhattan apartment with its lone brave basil plant on the window ledge. If Meg could have her little garden in a 300-square-foot apartment in Manhattan, so can you—assuming you don't live in a windowless closet.

There's something soothing about having plants around, especially plants that are going to spice up your life and your health, so that little basil plant was not only a culinary accoutrement for Meg—it was a personification of health and well-being.

The other myth to debunk is that gardening is difficult and a lot of hard work. The truth is, it's as hard as you make it. In this chapter, you'll get some ideas that make gardening unbelievably easy and rewarding.

Like humans, plants need air, light, water, and food. It's not a magic formula; it's just simple common sense. It's really as easy as that. A plant that has the right nutrients and all the other necessities of life (sun, water, and air) will be strong. And a strong plant has built-in protection against disease and against many insect predators. As with human physiology, prevention is the best route.

The Basics

Light: Most vegetables, fruit, and herb crops need a minimum of six hours of direct sunlight a day. Watch your proposed garden site and chart its daily sunlight. Now is a great time to start a garden journal if you don't already have one. I keep my journal on my computer with a separate file for each year, but if you're less technologically oriented, a looseleaf binder is a good choice so you can easily add in interesting articles, photos, etc.

Water: I'm not very scientific about this, but I like to be sure my vegetables get at least an inch of water a week. I keep a couple of old cat food cans in the garden to measure the amount if I am using the sprinkler. In really dry years, I set up soaker hoses and run them for an hour every other day. I also have a fancy-pants electronic rain gauge (which I love!) that tells me exactly how much rain we are getting. I enter the monthly totals in my garden journal. Much lower tech, but just as easy, is to stick your finger in the soil to gauge the moisture. If the soil is moist an inch down, your plants are fine. If it's dry more than an inch down, they need water.

Air: Overcrowding is a sure invitation for disease. This is something to watch out for if you only have space for a square foot garden, especially if you are in an area with humid, hot summer days and nights that promote fungal growth. If your garden is in a place where there is little air circulation, plant your crops farther apart to give them a little more breathing room.

Food: Of course, all plants need food. Nutritious soil, side dressing with compost, and the occasional "dessert" of a specific nutrient you might need should keep most plants healthy. Herbs, on the other hand, are largely Mediterranean in origin—think hot and dry in rocky soil. Fertilizer, or even any more than a passing handful of compost once a year, may actually harm them. Fruit trees and bushes are another matter entirely and, since they have individual needs, you'd do best to research them in depth. In any case, it's a good idea to have your soil analyzed once a year so you'll know exactly what it needs. In most states, the Cooperative Extension Service can do this for you inexpensively or even free.

Be Open to Experimentation

I'm not a very scientific gardener, although I do keep a garden journal detailing when I plant, major additions to the landscapes (trees, etc.), rainfall, and most important, my failures. You should try to do the same. It should help you learn from mistakes and successes as you move from one season to the next.

I'm an experimenter, usually for emotional rather than scientific reasons. Why wouldn't it be wonderful to have moonflowers (a personal passion) climbing my pea trellises after the pea harvest is finished? It would be lovely. Well, there's a good reason why not. The moonflowers shaded the beans and that was the end of the beans. Next time, maybe I can intentionally use them to shade lettuce and spinach to keep cool-weather crops from bolting (sending up seed stalks, which makes the leaves bitter) in hot weather.

My enthusiasm is often eclipsed by harsh reality. As much as I love cantaloupes, I have a black thumb when it comes to growing them. I have finally accepted the fact that there is some karmic reason why I am to be denied cantaloupes from my garden.

I encourage you to be an experimenter, too. Some of your experiments will fail, but just as many will succeed and some will be big winners. It's worth the journey!

Small-Space Gardening

Back to that pesky issue of space . . . whether you only have an apartment balcony or you only want to grow a few tomatoes, container gardening is the way to go. There are lots of choices of containers, and even urban gardeners can find sources for everything they need. With the Internet, the choices are virtually unlimited.

I like to have cherry tomatoes close at hand, so I bought two 4-foot-long plastic planter boxes with reservoirs a few years back. I can plant two tomato plants in each one and support the plants by tying them to the porch rail.

I love the convenience of having them right there for a quick lunch, and the three-gallon water reservoirs keep them from drying out even if I'm away for a few days.

The need for lots of water is always an issue with containerized plants because the evaporation rate is very high. With regular planters, you may need to water daily just to be sure they don't dry out and get stressed. Stress will eventually weaken any plant, leaving it vulnerable to insects and diseases and reducing crop yields.

The soil for containerized plants is very important. Regular garden soil, even compost, is usually too dense for container gardening. You might try a mixture of equal parts compost, vermiculite, and peat moss (often used in square foot gardening). I generally use the varieties of organic potting mix that are now readily available.

QUICK TIP

I love the look of clay pots, but be aware that they deteriorate over time. They'll split and, because they are porous, water trapped inside will cause them to crack and peel if they are left outside in the winter. They are also more permeable, so you need to water plants more often and take extra care when cleaning and disinfecting them in the spring in case there are any residual disease organisms. You can use clay pots as cache-pots for plants grown in plastic pots. Just be sure to put your clay pots away in winter.

The sky is the limit when it comes to the containers you can use for your mini-garden. Just be sure they have good drainage and they can support stakes if you're growing a crop that needs staking, like tomatoes.

Community Gardens

A community garden is a shared space where a group of people or residents of a certain area grow their vegetables. More and more city neighborhoods are starting community gardens on empty lots in the center of a city, in local parks, and on private properties that are donated for this purpose. These gardens can be funded through local governments, community services, or specific groups. The main purpose is to make space available for growing food for everyone who wants to take part. You can check out your local area for an existing community garden or look into starting one in your neighborhood. You can get lots of excellent information from the American Community Gardening Association, *www.communitygarden.org.*

Community Supported Agriculture (CSA)

A community supported agriculture (CSA) program is usually started by a farmer who decides to grow vegetables for a group of people who sign up to receive a certain amount of food each week during the growing season.

Being a member of the CSA may mean volunteering at the farm to help out with planting, weeding, and harvesting the vegetables. This is a great way for you and your family to spend a few days a month helping to grow the food you receive from the CSA every week. The website *www.localharvest.org/csa* allows you to find participating farms in your area.

Raised Beds

Raised beds are my favorite form of garden for several reasons:

1. They keep the garden looking neat. You can even be creative and make angled beds or whatever suits your taste.
2. They keep weeds from the paths out of the garden proper.
3. They're a great source of rich soil—I add horse manure, compost, and shredded leaves for a loamy mixture that my plants love. It's far more fertile than ordinary garden soil.
4. They're bottomless, so roots can grow as far down as they need.
5. They're easy to weed, since you never step into the soil and therefore it stays loose. A few strokes with a hoe usually take care of any tilling you might need in the spring.

The only real downside of raised beds is that they may require more water in dry climates.

You can make raised beds out of a wide variety of materials. Some of mine are made from ancient railroad ties that once graced my friend Sharon's gardens. Others are made from some composite 6x6 timbers, made of wood and shredded tires, that the garden center was selling a few years back. They are supposed to last for 75 years, so I probably won't be around to see if that is true. Sadly, these now seem to be unavailable.

The best materials for your raised beds are simple 1x8 or, better yet, 2x8 lumber. The depth is your choice, although it should be a minimum of 6 inches. If you have limited mobility, you can build the beds as deep as you like. You can even make them waist high so you can work without bending, or even while sitting in a chair. Just remember, it will take much more soil to fill them.

> **WARNING:**
> Don't make raised beds out of newer railroad ties because they are saturated with toxic creosote. Ditto for treated lumber, which has been treated with copper-based preservatives that you wouldn't want around your food crops.

Your best bet is to plan on creating beds that are no more than 4 feet wide (assuming you can walk all the way around them) so you can easily reach in to plant, weed, and harvest without stepping in the bed and compacting the soil. An 8-foot length is easily manageable, but there's no reason why you can't make the beds any length you like.

To create raised beds, simply lay out the boards in the shape you like and, using at least four 3-inch wood screws per joint, screw the pieces together and set them in place on top of soil from which you've removed all grass and weeds. If your bed is larger than 4' x 8', you may need to add a crossmember for stability since the soil will push outward on the joints.

Over time, since you shouldn't use treated lumber, your raised bed timbers will rot and need to be replaced. Wood that is in contact with soil rots more quickly, so you might consider stapling some heavy plastic on the bottom of the lumber to increase its longevity. Depending on the moisture levels of your soil, you'll probably need new beds every three to five years. If you stagger your replacement schedule, you'll minimize your yearly cost and labor.

Square Foot Gardening

Mel Bartholomew, a brilliant engineer, developed this method of gardening in the '80s in answer to the traditional and inefficient row-type gardening. I experimented with square foot gardening a few years back and found many pros and cons. I continue to use the method in a limited sense.

In a nutshell, here's how it works. Start with a typical raised bed 6 inches deep (a 4' x 4' bed is easiest to work with). Build a grid of 1-foot squares (I used scrap wood that had been ripped to 1-inch widths for another project) and attach it to your raised bed frame. In a 4' x4' bed, this will give you sixteen squares to work with.

If the bed is going to set on the ground, line the bottom with landscape cloth to prevent mixing the native soil and the special soil you will be using, and to keep all weeds out. If you've built a raised bed on legs (as I did for experimental purposes) you'll need to provide a plywood bottom with holes drilled for drainage, as well as substantial reinforcement to the bottom. The soil becomes very heavy when it is wet, as I discovered to my chagrin the first year, when the entire bottom fell out, landing plants and soil on the ground. I blithely turned it over (picture an upside-down table) and found that the legs provided a handy-dandy support for floating row covers and for protection against frost in the spring and fall.

Fill the bed with equal parts peat moss, vermiculite, and composted vegetable matter and manure. This can be a bit more work, but this combo supposedly never needs to be replaced, only replenished with a scoop of compost here and there. At about the halfway point, stop and give it a complete soaking with your hose. Wait an hour or two before filling the bed to the top and soaking it again.

Plant densely—plan on planting one pepper or tomato per square foot, or eight beans or nine beets or sixteen radishes or carrots. When plants germinate, it is very easy to tell the weeds from the seedlings, so it's easy to keep the beds neat. When a square is empty (you've harvested it), simply replant with another crop and add a trowelful of compost. That's all there is to it!

MY ADVENTURE IN SQUARE FOOT GARDENING: A CAUTIONARY TALE

After some intensive self-examination, I concluded that my gardens are primarily for three crops: tomatoes, cucumbers, and peppers, in that order. I was completely unwilling to risk that my square foot garden might fail, and horror of horrors—I would have NO tomatoes, cukes, or peppers.

So I decided to conduct a controlled experiment. I would plant two 4' x 8' raised beds with my usual methods, and three beds with what I had begun to regard as "Mel's method." I would buy tomato and pepper plants from my favorite nursery and divide the plantings between the two methods.

I would use the same varieties in Mel's beds and my control beds. I'd even divide the plants within the individual flats to be sure there was no bugaboo that would jigger my results. I used cucumber seeds from the same packet in each bed to further establish my control.

In May, I eagerly planted, hoping I'd discovered a panacea and that I had forever left behind my least favorite gardening task: weeding on blistering July days when intruding weeds threaten to choke my veggies. I built fence supports on the north end of my beds for the tomatoes.

Everything that was going to germinate did so on cue. It all looked good. Of course, I had to replant a few things. I had added beans, lettuce, spinach, onions, peas, and some herbs to Mel's beds. They looked wonderful. Of course, the control beds also still looked good early in the season. I got an excellent harvest of peas that climbed up the trellis attached to one of the square foot beds.

Come June, the wild growing season began. This applies not only to plants I want but is actually more applicable to weeds. Go away for a week in June at your peril. Your garden will become a jungle overnight. Then the difference became very apparent. Both plants had weeds, but it was easier to stay ahead of the unwanted growth in the square foot beds because I could easily see the sprouts that didn't belong. That was pretty much the extent of the good news. That year was a heavy rain year and the first problem was that the soil mixture in Mel's beds began to compact. By mid-July, some of the squares had only 4 inches of soil. I added a little compost and tried to mound soil around my struggling tomatoes and peppers. By that time, the tomato and pepper plants were only half the size of the ones in the control beds, where I had already started to reap a modest harvest. Clearly, there simply wasn't enough root room for the tomatoes and peppers in Mel's beds.

The plants in those beds had also begun to crowd each other mercilessly. Cucumbers began to succumb to powdery mildew, even while their cousins next door thrived. I attributed that to lack of air circulation. Meanwhile, beans, spinach, and lettuce were doing just fine in the same beds. They're shallow-rooted, so the compacted soil didn't seem to have interfered with their growth. Through the next month, the tomatoes and peppers limped along in Mel's beds. The plants were spindly and weak. They did produce some very small fruit, but in far smaller quantities than their cousins in the raised beds.

My conclusion? Square foot gardening ain't all it's cracked up to be. It works well for shallow-rooted crops but it doesn't work well for sprawling crops; the plants become too crowded and the beds aren't deep enough to sustain root systems for strong plants and a good yield.

Traditional Row Gardens

There's something to be said for tradition, never mind that row gardens as we know them today are actually a reflection of the way field crops are planted by necessity.

Think of a field of corn or wheat: If the rows weren't straight and uniform, it would be difficult to plant, even more difficult to control weeds, and next to impossible to harvest.

The biggest upside of row gardens is that, unlike raised beds, you can easily use a tiller on them.

Yet, none of that is the case for the average 20' x 20' vegetable garden. Your goals in that case would be to maximize yield for the space and minimize the work required to plant, maintain, and harvest. It is nice if the garden is attractive, and even nicer if you have well-manicured garden paths.

Traditional row gardens don't fill that bill, but raised beds, container gardens, and even square foot gardens, or a mixture of all three, can certainly do so.

Garden Paths

Whether you've chosen raised beds, traditional rows, or any other type of garden plan, you'll need paths somewhere so you can have access to your plants for planting, weeding, and harvesting.

Three-foot-wide paths are ideal—if they are any narrower, it will be very difficult to get through, much less to manipulate a wheelbarrow or garden cart or carry containers for your gleanings or any of the tools you might need. They should be even wider if you plan to drive a garden tractor or navigate it with a lawn mower. In addition, there should be a path on each side of every 4-foot bed, whether it is a traditional row or raised bed, so you can have access to both sides of the bed.

What should you use to cover those paths? Bark mulch is neat, makes for easy walking, and is easily accessible in most areas. Put landscape cloth under the mulch to keep weeds down. The landscape cloth lasts for years, and even though the mulch will eventually break down and become compost itself, you can easily rake it aside and replace it every few years. Some other options include using thick layers of old newspaper or cardboard. They'll easily last for a year, maybe even two—and best of all, they're free. The downside is that they have to be replaced often and they don't look very pretty.

For a few years, I used shredded leaves, an abundant commodity in my neighborhood, but I found they broke down very quickly, enriching the soil and encouraging more weeds to take root.

Keeping Down the Weeds in Your Beds

The battle of the weeds is never-ending. I've never known anyone who can completely banish weeds. I always laugh when I read garden book or articles that suggest that after a few years of gardening in the same place, you will have removed all the weed roots and so they won't be as much of a problem as at the beginning.

Nonsense! Weeds are a fact of life. Not only do they magically appear in your beds, their seeds blow in on the wind and birds help in planting them. Give up on the idea that weeds will ever disappear from your garden or your life. Instead, consider these facts when deciding how to configure your garden:

- Container gardens are fairly easy to keep weed-free because you have so little space to worry about.
- Square foot gardening is a good way to minimize weeds—or at least to catch them early because of the easily identifiable pattern in which you are planting.
- Raised beds are the next best thing for weed control because you won't have to worry about edging.
- Traditional row gardens are the hardest to keep weeded.

So why bother weeding at all? Weeds are unsightly, but that's not why you want to keep them out of your garden. Most weeds are nutrient hogs, so they literally grab the nutrients in the soil that your plants need. Weeds are also water hogs, so they take away the water your plants need and can leave them weakened. Some weeds also attract insects, making your garden plants more vulnerable to insect attacks.

Hand-pulling the weeds is the old-fashioned way, tedious but sure. If you do a good job of tilling the soil before you plant, any weeds that take root should be easy to remove before they get too big.

Mulches

Ruth Stout popularized the no-dig approach to gardening in *How to Have a Green Thumb Without an Aching Back*. In this method of gardening, several inches of mulch are spread on garden beds and replenished every year. The mulch helps conserve water, keeps the weeds under control, and decomposes over time, enriching the garden soil. Vegetables are planted through or under the mulch. Keep in mind that the mulch shouldn't touch plant stems, because deep mulches can harbor diseases, especially fungi.

Shredded leaves make a great garden mulch. They are nearly perfect: They keep the weeds down; unlike straw, they have no seeds of their own; they hold the moisture in; and they compost themselves over a season so they amend the existing soil. However, shredded leaves can contribute to the acidity of your soil, so you may need to compensate by adding alkaline compost.

Spoiled hay is another common mulch. As spoiled as the hay might be, however, there are always still viable seeds and they create a terrible weed problem. Scratch that method off your list.

Old newspapers are great weed inhibitors, even if they are a bit unsightly. Of course, you could cover the newspapers with a thin layer of a more attractive mulch. A thick layer will last for a season and weeds can't permeate the layers, but water easily passes through.

Some people use landscape cloth in their garden beds, planting only in holes cut specifically for the plants. Some of these landscape cloths can last for years, and they effectively keep weeds down and let water pass through. The downside is that it's difficult to till the soil underneath and crop rotation is more difficult.

If you live in a very dry climate, mulching may be the only way you can keep the water near your plants where they need it.

Watering

Watering can be a big challenge, depending on the needs of your plants and the water situation where you live. If you're a Californian, you have the luxury of year-round gardening, but you may be on severe water restrictions. Wherever you live, there are always tradeoffs.

Your garden needs about an inch of water a week, preferably not all at once. Ideally, it should get about ⅓ of an inch three times a week. It's probably a pipe dream to rely on Mother Nature for such a regular rain schedule, so watering becomes necessary.

Hand-watering with your trusty $4 watering can is the cheapest, and most labor-intensive, way to quench your garden's thirst. If your garden isn't too large, this method works fine and you can be very sure of the amount of water your plants receive.

For maximum water conservation with minimum effort, soaker hoses work well. I put them in place at planting time, threading them around plants from bed to bed and turning them on with a mechanical timer for an hour at a time every other day. The soaker hoses deliver water right at the plant's base, where it goes into the soil rather than evaporating.

If you live in a water-rich area that is relatively windstill, by all means, just use a sprinkler. Just be aware that even in this situation, quite a bit of the water will blow away or evaporate. If you live in an extremely dry climate, you might want to consider an underground irrigation system that drips water directly to the plants' roots.

In any case, a timer attached to the hose spigot helps in case you tend to forget to turn off the hose! You can even get programmable timers that will turn on daily when you are away.

Fertilizing

Because I'm not of the precise and scientific school of gardening, I'm not as good as I should be at fertilizing. I do use an organic fertilizer system that contains, among other things, some really smelly fish meal and other goodies that help keep my plants healthy. I just have to remember to use it—which I do about once a month. I think the package instructions say to use it every couple of weeks in the growing season, but once a month works for me and my plants.

Compost can also replenish your soil. More about compost follows, but at this point it's simply important to know that compost adds to the nutrient levels of the soil and helps keep the plants healthy, and their immune systems strong.

To determine the levels of nutrients in your soil, do a simple soil test. Most states have county Cooperative Extension offices where you can have soil tests done. This is a free service in some states. Generally, a soil test will determine your soil pH (acidity or alkalinity); the percentage of organic matter (garden soil usually contains about 95 percent of all soil nitrogen, nitrate, and nitrogen that is soluble and usable by your plants); the presence of essential minerals as well as phosphorus, potassium, zinc, iron, and lime; and soil texture. This snapshot of your soil will tell you if additions are needed.

GROWING ORGANICALLY AND SOIL, PLANT HEALTH, AND PESTS

For some reason, many people have the notion that growing organically means you do not use fertilizer, insecticides, or disease control. This couldn't be further from the truth. Growing organically means that you employ *nontoxic means* of achieving the ends of general soil and plant health to repel pests and treat plant diseases.

The USDA has issued regulations for the fertilizers, pesticides, herbicides, and disease treatments that are accepted in order for a product to be sold commercially as certified organic. Since most of you aren't growing commercial crops, it's up to you, but the more natural you keep your garden, the healthier you will be, and you'll have a healthy wildlife population as well. If you truly do need them, you can find excellent nontoxic fertilizers, pesticides, and herbicides. I've listed my favorite sources in the Resources section.

Composting

There's no shortage of info on the myriad ways to compost—but the bottom line is that even the least scientific methods will render something that will improve the quality of your soil. We compost all of our household scraps except meat, cheese, and things like pasta. We also compost all of our yard and garden waste except diseased plant material.

You'll find a slew of books that tell you to layer your compost, perhaps starting with a 6-inch layer of grass clippings, then some food scraps, then some dry material like leaves.

That's not very realistic for most of us. I don't know about you, but I almost never have grass clippings and dry leaves at the same time. And it would be rare for me to have a huge amount of household scraps at once, too.

So here's my method: Everything goes into the bin at once! Watermelon rinds are covered up by weeds pulled from the gardens. Prunings from the trees and bushes are piled on top of avocado and peach pits, corn cobs, banana peels, leftover salad, and coffee grounds (which are great for the compost pile!). I have no idea where the authors of these scientific composting programs think we can keep this stuff until we have enough for a 6-inch layer in the bin. It would get pretty ripe in the summer heat before that day arrives.

So I toss it all in. Whenever I have it, it goes in.

Because in the end, compost happens. It needs little help. Sure, if you're in an all-fired hurry to get compost in six weeks, you'd need to take the temperature of the pile and rotate it and do all sorts of other shenanigans, but assuming you're not in a hurry, you can let Mother Nature take a year or two to make that black gold.

Here's a unique system of compost bins that costs nothing and is very effective. Go to your local hardware store and take half a dozen wooden pallets off their hands. They're glad to give them away because they have to pay to have them removed. The wood is good and solid. Look for the best pallets and keep ones that are aesthetically pleasing. That's not really hard. The finished product actually looks pretty in the garden.

Here's what you'll need for each bin. You'll probably want two or three, depending on the size of your gardens, for reasons we'll explore later:

- Five pallets per bin; six for lids for your bins containing older compost
- Four cinder blocks
- Eight 30-inch lengths of rope

Here's how to construct the bins—without the use of a single nail, much less a hammer! It's up to you to figure out the most convenient place for your bins, whether close to the garden or closer to the house. It's a good idea to have them on level ground, but that's not even an absolute.

1. Make a base of four cinder blocks and set your strongest pallet on top of them. Having the base slightly raised will speed up the process somewhat because of increased air circulation to the pile.
2. Stand your four pallets on their edges on top of the base pallet. You may need a helper just to help you hold them.
3. Tie the pallets together at the top and bottom corners using the rope.

That's it. Now you have a square bin in which you can just pile your waste materials. The bin is well aerated from below and from the slatted sides. When you want to open it, simply untie the corner ropes and remove the vertical pallets.

Turn the compost if you like. Or not. The process will be slightly faster if you turn your compost.

After the first year, you may want to build a second bin into which you could transfer the uncomposted materials from the first bin. The sixth pallet serves as a lid for the first bin, so no more material is accidentally added to the nearly finished compost. Then you have an empty first bin so you can add any and all compostable materials throughout the season. If you have a large volume, you may want a third bin.

Over time your pallets will weaken and fall apart, but they should last for about four years. A trip to the local hardware store is all you need to do to replace them.

The total one-time cost for this two-bin compost system: about $25. The cinder blocks and rope will last indefinitely. I've been using the same ones for about ten years now.

Frost Protection

Two years ago, I ate the last fresh tomato from my garden on December 1. The high temperature that day was 33 degrees and the low somewhere in the low 20s. What a rare pleasure!

Most who live in cool climates would love to extend the growing season. You can do it! The degree to which you'll be able to keep things growing past killing frost is partly due to your energy, the health of your plants, and the severity of your winter.

- **If you're really serious,** a heated greenhouse will be successful in almost any climate. **If you're moderately serious,** some simple cold frames may provide you with lettuce and other cool-weather crops through a good part of the winter.
- **If you're pretty casual,** throw an old sheet over your tomatoes for the first few frosts and harvest your green tomatoes before the first hard frost. Set them in your windowsill and hope for the best. Probably about half of them will ripen over time.
- **If you're scientific about your garden,** you can create row covers from bent poly plumbing pipe with Reemay or other fabric clothespinned to the frames.

THE CHILLY LETTUCE THAT COULD

I grow winter lettuce in my cold frames—constructed very simply with a few cinder blocks, a couple of old storm windows (bought for next to nothing at the local thrift store), and some pretty lame sides constructed from scrap wood. They face south, and the back side is higher than the front side so the window, just set atop the blocks, sits at an angle. The scrap wood pieces fill in the open sides. It is far from airtight and, in theory, should not be very effective in extreme temperatures.

In the mountains of North Carolina, we had one of the worst winters on record in 2009–2010. Snow followed by ice storm, followed by more snow and ice and unrelenting temperatures in the teens and single digits. Because the small embankment leading to my garden became a six-inch-thick ice slide, I did not visit my garden for six weeks. I never watered the winter lettuce, and the storm windows were iced over for weeks on end. I was sure there was no lettuce.

When the first thaw came, I eagerly made my way through the slush to check my cold frames, to find them crammed full of leafy green goodness!

My takeaway: Perhaps benign neglect and good thoughts are more important to the success of winter lettuce than TLC.

CHAPTER 4

Preparing for Your Garden

Growing a vegetable garden will take effort and time, so it is important to grow what you and your family will eat—as well as the foods that will help you feel healthy and vibrant. As you see in Part I, there are *always* foods you can eat for what ails you! So I encourage you to try something new, especially if it will contribute to your well-being. If you embark on this adventure, you'll quickly see that there's nothing like eating a vegetable fresh from your garden. The flavor is far superior to anything you buy at the grocery store, so you might be surprised by what you or your family may enjoy eating!

In the unlikely event that you don't like something you grow or you have an abundance of one vegetable (commonly known as a bumper crop), give some away to friends, neighbors, or your community food bank. That can also make you feel good!

Step by Step

Planting a vegetable garden can be very rewarding. It is miraculous how a tiny little seed can produce enough nourishing vegetables to feed your family for several meals. By growing just one or two vegetables for yourself, you can not only fortify your health, but also save on trips to the supermarket, understand exactly what is in your food, and control how it was grown.

Size

Whatever your reason for growing your own vegetables, it is important to consider that gardening does take time, money, and energy. Be realistic when you estimate how much time you have to devote to your garden. People will often start a huge garden in the spring only to tire of it and let the weeds take over by summer.

If you are a first-time gardener, start small. Increase the size of your site every year as you become more familiar with growing your own vegetables. If you only have a few minutes a day to spend on your vegetable garden, perhaps you can start with a few pots. If you have a few hours a week, you could manage a small garden spot or perhaps a raised bed. If you want to grow enough food to feed your family all year round, you may need to set aside at least one day a week to tend to a much larger garden. No matter where you live, you can find a spot to grow some of your own vegetables.

Consider Your Climate

The first step is to consider your climate zone. The United States and Canada are divided into plant hardiness zones that range from 1—the coldest areas such as Alaska—up to 11—the warmest areas such as southern California, southern Florida, and Hawaii. These zones are based on temperature variations and first and last frost dates, which give the gardener an idea of what plants will grow best in each zone.

These zones can be important when choosing perennial plants, but most vegetables are annuals, and so as long as you grow your crops during the appropriate season for your hardiness zone, your vegetable garden won't be seriously affected by zone. Most areas in the United States and Canada also have four seasons, and the majority of gardeners grow vegetables in the spring and summer, although some gardeners in the southern United States can grow during the fall and winter months as well. Your growing season can be extended by using greenhouses or other structures to give vegetable plants protection, not only from frost, but also from wind and hailstorms.

The length of your growing season will be pretty standard from year to year but can vary depending on the weather. Learn the frost-free dates in your area. Master Gardeners (sponsored by county offices of your state's Cooperative Extension Service) are usually a wealth of information and can advise you. Be aware, however, that frost-free dates are simply averages. Here in the mountains, our traditional spring planting date is May 15, but one year we had a killing frost on Memorial Day. Also be aware of the average amount of rainfall in your area when choosing your site if you need extra good drainage in high rainfall areas or if you need a lower site that will collect rainwater if you live in a dry climate.

While the general climate of your area is important to consider, each garden site also will have specific issues. For example, is the area protected from the wind? Does the site have lots of mature trees that will block out the sun, or does it get full sun? Note: Pay attention to the trees in their fully leafed-out condition. You may find the shade situation is very different in full summer from what it is in early spring.

> **GARDENING IS GOOD FOR YOUR HEALTH—IN MORE WAYS THAN ONE!**
>
> In addition to reaping the nutritional benefits from what you grow, you can burn 150–250 calories per hour just by getting out into your vegetable garden. Exercise also releases endorphins into the bloodstream. Endorphins make you feel happy and give you a more positive outlook overall. Sign me up!

What Do You Want to Grow?

When choosing a garden site, it is important to know what you would like to grow. Some vegetables need warmth and lots of sunlight to grow, while others do well in a shadier spot.

Planning what you want to grow will save you time, money, and energy in the long run. Write down a list of vegetables that you love to eat. Get your family involved so they can be part of the decision-making process. That way, they'll feel a sense of ownership and just might be more willing to help plant and take care of the garden.

Then add in a couple of things you wouldn't ordinarily grow, just for fun. If you've never grown rutabagas or turnips or kale, give them a try. They are delicious, especially when they are very fresh.

Children love to garden. For young children, choose quick-growing veggies like radishes so they can watch them grow. Veggies that are fun to eat, like peas or corn, are also great. Let older children grow what they want in their own designated little garden. Teach them how to plant, weed, water, and take care of that area.

Some vegetables take a lot more of your time than others, so take that into account when you make your selections:

Swiss chard and salad greens are easy to grow and can be harvested several times from just a few plants.

A 20-foot row of asparagus will take some time to plant initially, but you'll be able to look forward to enjoying asparagus every spring for years to come.

Some root crops, such as carrots, beets, or radishes, need to be thinned as they grow. This can be time consuming, especially if you have large rows of these vegetables. It is important to know how much time you want to put into gardening. The good news: You can put your thinnings into a salad.

If you want to grow enough of certain vegetables so that you can preserve or freeze them for eating during the winter months, plan ahead and plant more than you would need for fresh eating alone.

If space is a consideration, research plants that give bigger yields but don't take up a lot of space. Root crops (except potatoes) and leafy greens will yield a lot for the space they use up. You can train tomatoes, cucumbers, and beans to grow vertically, giving you more of a harvest for the space used. Consider growing vegetables that have more than one edible part. For example, if you grow beets, you can eat the root and enjoy the leaves in a salad. If you grow onions, you can eat the greens in your salad and then wait until the bulbs are big enough to harvest.

Here is a list of ten common vegetables you can easily grow. Not coincidentally, they are among our top healing foods:

- Beans
- Cabbage
- Carrots
- Cucumbers
- Lettuce
- Onions
- Peas
- Potatoes
- Squash
- Tomatoes

The Importance of Sunlight

Sunlight plays a big part in growing a successful vegetable garden. This is the one area in which you have the least control. Most vegetables need an average of six hours of direct sunlight in order to grow. If you only have a shadier spot, you'll find there are a few plants that will grow in a bit of shade. Consider growing the most sun-loving vegetables in containers that you can move around to follow the sun's path.

The sun alters its path throughout the seasons, so take the time to track its progress. Keep track of the time when sunlight hits your garden spot throughout the different seasons and record how long it stays in full sun. It probably won't matter if your garden site is deprived of sunlight in the winter, since in most of the country you won't be growing anything at that time, but if you are sunlight deficient during the spring and summer, you will need to choose another site.

You also want to consider how the trees in the area affect the amount of sun your site will receive. You may get full sun in the winter months when the leaves are off the trees, but the site becomes shadier as the leaves come out.

The following vegetables do well with four to six hours of direct sunlight a day:

- Carrots
- Lettuce
- Kale
- Peas
- Swiss chard

The following vegetables traditionally produce fruit and need more sun, at least six hours of sunlight (better yet, eight hours):

- Cucumbers
- Eggplants
- Peppers
- Squash
- Tomatoes

Consider whether your vegetable plants will have any competition for the soil's nutrients. Perennial shrubs aren't usually a problem, and they can even benefit your garden by attracting beneficial insects to the vegetable patch. But beware of planting your garden near large trees, which will take nutrients from your vegetable plants.

If you have an area that gets a lot of sun—six hours or more—most vegetables will grow well. If your garden site gets a lot of heat, choose vegetables that grow best in hot conditions. Most of these vegetables are often started indoors in the early spring and planted out at the end of May or in June, depending on your climate.

The following are some warm-season or heat-loving vegetables:

- Beans
- Corn
- Cucumbers
- Eggplants

- Okra
- Peppers
- Squash
- Sweet potatoes
- Tomatoes

The Length of Your Growing Season

If you live in an area where you have a very short growing season—for example, from June to September such as you would find in zones 4 and 5 across the northern border of the United States—you must take that into account. There are some vegetables that grow very quickly from seed, like radishes and some salad greens that mature in 30 to 45 days.

Other vegetables, like tomatoes, peppers, and melons, need three to four months or more to grow from seed to maturity. These vegetables are most often started from seed in greenhouses and transplanted once the weather is warm enough. This gives them the head start they need to mature, especially if you get your first frost in September, as you might if you are USDA zone 4 in northern New England and the northern parts of the Plains states.

If you live in an area with a long growing season where you can plant seeds in March and harvest as late as November and December (USDA zones 8, 9, and 10, the deep South, California and the coastal regions of the Pacific Northwest), consider succession planting so you can eat your vegetables through most of the year. If you live in this kind of climate, you can plant cool-season crops such as radishes, leeks, onions, salad greens, and spinach early in March, warm-season crops at the end of May, and another round of cool-season crops of broccoli, Brussels sprouts, cabbage, and kale in late summer for fall harvesting.

When you choose which vegetables you want to grow, take the time to learn more about your climate and garden conditions. This is an important step toward having a successful and bountiful vegetable harvest.

Consider What the Veggies Need

You also need to know the individual needs of the types of vegetable plants you have chosen to grow. Some vegetable plants grow best upright or vertical; others like to be protected from the wind, rain, or hot sun. All of these factors need to be considered when planning your vegetable garden layout.

Vertical Support

Growing certain plants vertically is great, especially if you are short on space or want the plants to give you some privacy. Vertical planting can also add structure and interest to your vegetable garden. Most important, growing vertically is crucial for the health of some plants. Tomatoes that are left to grow along the ground will mold, rot, and attract pests and diseases. Vertical planting also increases air circulation. Cucumbers like air around them. Keep in mind that you will need supports for plants that want to grow upward. There are several kinds of tomato cages on the market, and sometimes it's simple to plant your cucumber, beans, or peas near a fence or to put a piece of fencing in the garden bed.

Protection from the Elements

Some vegetables need lots of sun and warmth to grow, while others like it a bit shadier and cooler. Depending on your garden conditions, you may need to protect some of your plants from the elements. Early in the spring, young plants need to be protected from the cold and some pests. This can be done by throwing a light blanket, sheet, or floating row cover over the plant at night or during the hottest part of the day. A floating row cover, typically made of a lightweight translucent fabric attached to a variety of type of framework (plastic plumbing pipe bent in a U shape and inserted into the ground makes a good frame), can actually protect tender plants from both heat and cold as well as keep out insects. Similarly, in most climates except those farthest to the north, you can replant lettuce in early September and harvest through the fall if you use a floating row cover for protection from light frost. A slatted wooden structure also can shelter the plants.

If you get an unexpected cold spell in the spring and you've already planted your more tender crops, young transplants or seedlings will need a little extra protection. All it takes is an old bedsheet, newspaper, or cardboard box to keep your veggie plants protected from frost.

You already know how important it is to have easy access to your water source. You must also take into consideration different plants' watering needs. Some plants love their leaves to be wet, but others do better if their leaves are mostly dry. Watering overhead is great for greens, spinach, and lettuces; it keeps them cool and makes the leaves fresh and crisp for harvesting. Tomatoes and carrots can easily get blight and other diseases if their leaves get wet (of course, they'll get wet when it rains), so it is best to water these vegetables at the base of the plant. A drip irrigation system or a soaker hose provides an ideal solution. Another consideration is the size of the vegetable plant's leaves. If you are overhead sprinkling broccoli, cabbage, or squash, the leaves will hog the water and very little will reach the roots, where it is most needed.

Placement of the Plants

Unless you're doing a square foot garden, now is the time to get out graph paper, a ruler, and a pencil so you can plan your garden layout.

Planning ahead will save you money and time. With a detailed plan, you will purchase the seeds and transplants you need rather than wasting money by bringing home plants for which you don't have space or even a real need.

If you're a novice gardener, making a garden plan in advance will help you overcome uncertainty. If you don't know where to start, there's a good chance you might never get started at all. Having a garden layout will help you. It is easier to erase something on paper than it is to move around plants in your garden. Take your time with drawing up your plan. It's a wonderful activity for those cold winter days when the seed catalogs start arriving in the mail.

Use your graph paper and a pencil to draw your garden site to scale, making a note of the directions north, south, east, and west. You can even label the beds with the number of hours of direct sunlight. If possible, have your raised beds or rows facing north to south for best distribution of sunlight. Now divide your garden site into three sections—four if you are going to plant perennial vegetables. Label each section with a letter or number; this will help you plan your rotations year after year.

Vegetable rotation means you plant your vegetables in a different spot each year. Different vegetable plants require and use different amounts of nutrients and attract different pests and diseases, so rotation will help you grow a more successful garden and create healthier garden soil.

List the vegetables you are planning to grow and group them into three categories:

1. Root vegetables
2. Brassicas (broccoli, cauliflower, cabbage, Brussels sprouts)
3. Everything else

Make a note of each plant's space needs as it grows to maturity. (You will find information on specific vegetables in Chapter 5.) As you plan your layout, remember to use the correct spacing for each kind of vegetable and put the taller plants to the north side so they do not shade out the sun for the smaller ones, unless you want to shade some cool-weather crops, such as lettuce.

The Garden Soil

The types of weeds growing in your garden are a good indication of how good your soil is. Some common weeds that indicate you have rich soil are burdock, ground ivy, lamb's quarters, pigweed, and purslane. Some weeds that indicate you have poorly drained soil are curly dock, hedge bindweed, sheep sorrel, and smartweed.

Soil Preparation

Once you have your garden layout planned, it's time to prepare your garden beds. Start preparing your soil when it is dry enough in early spring. To test your soil for wetness, take a handful of soil and squeeze it in your hand. If it forms a ball, it is too wet. If it crumbles, the soil is ready to work.

Remove Any Grass

Remove any grass, rocks, or debris from the area where you'll be planting. If you are a first-time gardener, prepare a ten-foot-square area for rows or two raised beds with a two-foot walkway in between. If you start with a small area, you will less likely be overwhelmed and more likely to be successful with your harvest. You can always make the area larger each year as you get more experienced.

One of the easiest ways to remove grass in early spring is to place a heavy plastic tarp over the area and stretch it out on the ground using tent stakes or weighting the corners with bricks or stones. The grass underneath will be killed in about two weeks. Then you can easily rake it out and till the soil underneath.

Turn the Soil

You can turn the soil with a spade or more sophisticated equipment such as a rototiller or tractor and plow; it all depends on the size of your garden area. If you are just starting out with a small area, a spade is probably the easiest and cheapest method—although it can be back-breaking work, so take your time.

After turning the soil, take time to break down any large clumps that are left with a rake or hand cultivator and remove any rocks larger than a marble.

Apply Soil Amendments and Organic Fertilizers

Once you have tilled the soil in the early spring, add well-rotted manure and compost to your beds. Add at least ½" to give your soil a healthy structure and to improve fertility. Dig these organic amendments into the top 6 to 12 inches of your garden soil.

If you need to add lime or sulfur to your garden soil to increase or decrease the pH, do that separately from your soil amendments and fertilizers. You should add in these elements at least one week apart so they can all benefit your garden soil.

Now is also the time to add extra nitrogen, phosphorus, potassium, or lime if you need them. Refer to your soil test to determine your individual needs. All of these can be dug into the top few inches of the soil with either a spade or rake.

Rake the Bed

Once you have tilled and added in amendments and fertilizers, you want to get the bed ready for planting. Raking will make the bed smooth and level, and you can pick out any debris or small rocks you missed before. A soil with a consistency of coarse bread crumbs is best for planting your vegetables, especially if you are seeding directly. Taking the time to prepare your soil well will give you great vegetables to enjoy.

Starting Seeds Outdoors

There are two ways to plant your vegetable seeds: directly outdoors into the soil or indoors in seed trays to be transplanted to the garden later. Different vegetable seeds have different requirements for germination and maturing; some need heat and some do better in cool weather. You must know the best way to start each of your vegetables. Most vegetable seeds will do well either way, but some vegetables, such as root crops, need to be seeded directly because they do not grow well if their roots are disturbed.

Starting seeds indoors will give them a head start. This is beneficial, especially if you live in a cold climate where you cannot get into your garden until the end of May.

Vegetables best started by seeding directly into the soil include these:

- Beans
- Beets
- Carrots
- Corn

- Garlic
- Peas
- Potatoes
- Radish
- Rutabagas
- Salad greens

Vegetable seed packets give you valuable information about planting depths and spaces between plants. However, if you don't have the seed packet handy, a good rule of thumb is to plant the seed twice the depth of the size of the seed. Spacing between plants is determined by the final size of the plant, as you'll learn in Chapter 5.

When starting your seeds outdoors, make sure the conditions are right for your specific vegetable seed. If the soil is too wet and cold or too dry and hot, the seed may not germinate. Know what each variety of seed you are planting requires.

Here is a quick checklist for planting your seeds directly into your garden beds.

- Make sure the soil is moist, not wet.
- Mark the row using a stick, a string, the edge of a hoe, or your finger. It should be the depth recommended for that particular seed.
- Sow the seed. If the seed is small, like lettuce, take a pinch of seed with your fingers and then gently spread the seed in the area you marked. Larger seeds like beans or peas can be dropped into a row, or a pattern if you're using square foot gardening. Place them an appropriate distance apart as you go.
- Gently cover the seed with soil. You can do this by using your hand or the backside of a rake.
- Firm down the soil. This is done using your hand or the back of a hoe. This prevents the soil and seed from being blown away by wind or getting washed away when you water the bed.
- Water the bed. Seeds need to be moist to germinate, so gently spray water on the area you have just planted. Do not water too

heavily or quickly or you may wash the seeds away. You will need to keep the area well moistened until you see the first green shoots coming through the soil. After that, water when the soil ½ inch down is dry. Do not let the bed dry out.

- Thin the plants. Once the first green shoots appear, some vegetable plants, including carrots, radishes, turnips, spinach, and salad greens, need to be thinned. Thinning helps to make room for the vegetable plants to grow to maturity and gives you the ingredients for a delicious early spring salad.

Some vegetables, like tomatoes, peppers, and eggplant, are difficult to start outdoors because the seed needs a very specific temperature to germinate. These are best started indoors so you have more control over their growing conditions. You also can buy them as started plants at your local garden center.

Transplants: Start Your Own or Buy?

Growing your own seedlings can be a very satisfying part of vegetable gardening. Its advantages are many. It can be more economical, especially if you have a large garden; it gives you a head start with your growing season; and you'll know exactly how many plants you will have to transplant. In addition, starting your own seedlings may prevent diseases or pests from coming into your garden.

Starting Your Own Seedlings

The process of starting your own seedlings can be intimidating, but it can be easily accomplished with a little know-how. Start seeds indoors in flats.

Vegetables that do better started indoors and then transplanted to the garden include these:

- Broccoli
- Cabbage
- Cauliflower

- Celery
- Eggplants
- Lettuce
- Onions
- Peppers
- Tomatoes

Many nurseries or garden stores sell seed starter kits. They come with all the components needed to start your own transplants—a tray, cells, labels, and a clear plastic lid. The two most common sizes are sheets that have seventy-two cells and sheets with twenty-four cells. The larger the vegetable plants at maturity, the larger the flat you should use for growing the seedling. For example, lettuce is usually planted in the seventy-two-cell sheets, and brassicas or tomatoes are started in the twenty-four-cell sheets. The tray, cells, and lid can be reused from year to year, but make sure they are clean. Use one part bleach to ten parts water to clean them at the beginning of the season.

Some kits come with a starter mix, but you may have to purchase this separately. Use sterile potting soil made specifically for starting seeds; it is lighter weight than your garden soil.

Buying Transplants

If you do not have the time or desire to start you own seedlings, check your local nursery or garden center for vegetable transplants. Make sure you purchase your seedlings from a reputable business and choose their healthiest seedlings. Unhealthy transplants can easily introduce insects and disease to your garden. A healthy transplant is bushy and compact, not spindly or leggy. The stems should be a healthy color and strong. Avoid plants whose roots are showing through the drain holes. These plants may be root bound, which may prevent them from growing to their full potential. Make sure you are ready to set out your transplants into the garden as soon as you bring them home.

CHAPTER 5

Growing Your Vegetables

You may have read through the list of ailments that affect you and your family and skipped directly to this chapter, eager to grow the very best for your personal health conditions. If so, that's fine, although if you're a novice gardener, you might want to review some of the garden basics. In fact, I learned quite a bit about garden basics myself while I researched this book, even though I've been gardening for—ahem—more than 40 years. We can always learn something new!

ROTATING YOUR CROPS

Growing your veggie plants in a different area each year discourages pests and diseases in your soil. Each vegetable plant or family of plants requires different nutrients and attracts different pests and diseases. These pests usually remain in the soil right where the plant was grown, so by moving your plants to a new area of the garden, harmful organisms will be less likely to survive. A good rule of thumb is to rotate your crops so the varieties return to their original spot about once every four years.

So now you have your site selected, your plan on paper, your seeds in hand, and perhaps you've even started a few tomatoes or peppers. You've checked the frost-free date in your area and you're ready to go!

Here's what you need to know about each individual type of plant in order to get the best results:

COMPANION PLANTING

Companion planting helps to keep pests and diseases away from certain plants. In this method, certain plants are grown together so that they help each other. One plant may attract beneficial insects that will eat common pests, keeping the plants nearby healthier. Another plant may deter a pest, keeping the plant beside it healthier. Some plants don't get along well—like strawberries and broccoli or beans and peas with garlic, onions, and chives.

Asparagus

Asparagus is a perennial vegetable. Plant in a permanent area; once established, asparagus will produce new shoots each spring for fifteen to twenty years without too much work on your part. It is best to buy one-year-old male crowns or rhizomes, since it takes three years to grow this vegetable from seed to harvest. In the first year after planting, don't cut any of the spears; allow them to grow so the roots can gain strength. The feathery foliage will nourish the roots, which in turn will give you more spears in the second year. In the second year, you can harvest the first few spears, but stop harvesting once the spears start to look spindly or have a diameter less than ¼ inch. In the third and following years, you will be able to harvest over a much longer season.

Prepare the bed by digging in generous amounts of compost or aged manure. Dig a foot-deep trench and then fill it with 3 to 4 inches of organic material. Mix this with the existing soil. Lay the crowns in the trench and cover them with 2 inches of soil, but do not cover the tips of the shoots. As the plant grows, mound more soil around each plant.

In the fall, cut back the fernlike foliage. This is also a great time to mulch the bed with aged manure to add nutrients to the soil as it decomposes over the winter. Leaves or straw can be added on top for more protection from the cold.

QUICK TIPS FOR GROWING ASPARAGUS

Family name	Asparagaceae (lily family).
Edible parts	Young shoots called "spears."
Location	Full sun.
Best soil	Fertile, well-drained, sandy to clay loam soil; pH 6.0–6.7.
When to plant	Set out plants in spring when any danger of frost is past.
How to plant	Set out crowns 6 to 8 inches deep, 18 inches apart in rows spaced 3 to 5 feet apart. Cover the crown with 2 inches of soil and keep adding more soil as the plant grows.
How much to plant	10 plants per person
Companion plants	There are no other plants that have a positive effect, but avoid planting onions near asparagus, as they can have a negative effect.
Watering	Keep well watered.
Care	Cut back the foliage in the fall once it turns brown.
Fertilizing	Apply a high-nitrogen fertilizer twice a year, once when the spears emerge and again at the end of harvest. If you have a soil that has a pH lower than 6.0, apply lime in the spring as well.
Pests and diseases	Aphids and asparagus beetles.
When to harvest	Do not harvest the first year of planting. From the second year onward, harvest the spears when they are about the thickness of the diameter of a pencil and 6 to 8 inches high. Stop harvesting once the spears are thinner than the diameter of a pencil.
How to harvest	Cut the spear ½ inch below the soil. This will help to prevent any diseases.
Storage	Asparagus is best eaten fresh. It will keep in the refrigerator for about a week.

Beans

Beans are some of the tastiest of treats from the garden. They are easy to grow in pots or raised beds, can be trellised to add structure to your garden, and have lovely flowers that enhance the look of your garden! You sow the seeds directly into the garden, where at the right temperature they will germinate quickly and grow vigorously. Considering the small amount of space they take up in your garden, they produce real bounty. There are several different types of beans—bush beans (sometimes called snap beans), runner beans, pole beans, shelling beans for drying, lima beans, soybeans, and fava beans (sometimes called broad beans). Most varieties need warm soil to germinate, so they are usually planted in the late spring. To tell whether it's time to plant your beans, walk barefoot on the soil at midday. If it feels cold, hold off for a while. If it doesn't feel cold, you're ready to go. The exception to this is fava beans, which are a cool-weather bean and best planted in early spring.

QUICK TIPS FOR GROWING BEANS

Family name	Papilionaceae (pea or bean family).
Edible parts	Seeds and pods.
Location	Open, sunny area.
Best soil	Sandy, loamy soil; neutral pH.
When to plant	Seeds need a temperature of 70–90°F.
How to plant	Bush beans: Sow 1 inch deep, 3 inches apart in rows 18 to 24 inches apart, then thin to every 6 inches. Pole or runner beans: Plant 5 to 8 seeds to each stake; thin to 3 to 4 plants. For other types, check the seed packet for exact instructions.
How much to plant	Bush beans: 20 to 30 feet per person. Pole or runner beans: 20 to 25 feet per person. Dried beans: 100 feet per person.
Companion plants	Plant with beets, cabbage, carrots, corn, squash, and tomatoes. Plants that will have a negative effect are chives, fennel, garlic, and leeks.
Watering	Do not water seeds until they have sprouted, then water regularly after that.
Care	Set up stakes for pole or runners beans at the time of planting. To prevent the spread of disease, try not to touch the plants when they are wet.
Fertilizing	Fertilize with fish fertilizer or compost tea after the first heavy bloom and again when the pods are starting to form.
Pests and diseases	Aphids, leafhoppers, Mexican bean beetles, mites, damping off, and downy mildew are some common pests and diseases.

QUICK TIPS FOR GROWING BEANS

When to harvest	Depending on the variety, beans will be mature between 50 and 100 days. Check the specific varieties you choose to grow for more information. For bush varieties, harvest when the pod is still small, about 4 to 6 inches long. For fava beans, pick when the pods begin to drop with the weight of the seeds. Shell these and cook them like peas. Runner or pole beans are harvested when the pod is 6 to 10 inches long and still flat. Dried varieties are harvested when the pod is fully mature.
How to harvest	When you pick the pods, gently tug the pod with one hand while holding the plant so as not to pull out the whole plant.
Storage	Fresh beans will last for a week in the refrigerator. Beans can be blanched and frozen. They will keep in the freezer for several months. Dried beans will store for years if harvested and dried properly.

Beets

Beets are a love or hate vegetable; either you love them or you have no desire to eat them at all. They are great addition to any home garden because they are easy to grow, have a long harvest, take up a small amount of space in your garden, and can be stored. They have more than one edible part and can be eaten raw or cooked, so they are a very versatile vegetable. The young leaves are used with other baby greens in popular salad mixes. The mature leaves can be steamed for a nutritious side dish to add to any meal. The roots can be harvested as sweet and tender baby beets or they can be left to grow to maturity to be harvested as you need them all summer and fall.

The many variety of beets give you more options than just a round red beet. You can buy seeds that will produce elongated roots, which have a milder taste. Beets can now be grown in a multitude of colors. There are white, yellow, orange, and striped varieties.

Beets like a fairly rich soil that is free of rocks and debris. Add in aged animal manure and lime if needed when preparing your garden bed. Make sure your bed is well prepared with at least a foot of loose tilled soil for the roots to grow. Remove any lumps, rocks, or sticks from the soil so they don't impede the growth of the root. Beets are usually direct seeded to your garden bed; however, they are slow to germinate, so mark the bed where they are planted. The seed can produce more than one plant; they will need to be thinned so there is only one plant for every three to four inches of garden soil as the seedlings start to grow.

QUICK TIPS FOR GROWING BEETS

Botanical name	Chenopodiaceae (goose foot family).
Edible parts	Roots and tops.
Location	Sunny, open area.
Best soil	Fertile, well-drained soil, clean bed; pH 6.0–6.8.
When to plant	Sow April to mid-July for a continuous harvest.
How to plant	Sow seeds ½ inch deep and 1 inch apart in rows spaced 16 to 24 inches apart. Keep the soil moist until seeds have germinated; this can take from 14 to 21 days, so you need to be patient. Once the seedlings are a couple inches high, thin them so there is only 1 plant for every 3 inches of garden soil.
How much to plant	10 to 20 feet per person.
Companion plants	Cabbage has a positive effect on beets, so try to plant them near each other. Avoid planting beets near beans, because they can have a negative effect.
Weeding	Keep well weeded, especially when plants are small.
Watering	The soil needs to be kept moist when seeds are first planted. Once plants have sprouted, water regularly. If you are using an overhead sprinkler, make sure you leave it on long enough for the water to penetrate several inches into the soil in order to reach the roots.
Fertilizing	Dig in compost or aged animal manure and a balanced fertilizer when preparing the beds.
Pests and diseases	Leaf miners, beet web worms, flea beetles, wireworms, and leaf spot can affect your beet plants.
When to harvest	Beets mature in 45 to 65 days. You can start cutting the young leaves for salad when they are about 3 inches high. Start harvesting the roots once they reach the size of a golf ball. Harvest all your beets before the first frost in the fall.

QUICK TIPS FOR GROWING BEETS	
How to harvest	Cut the leaves individually or harvest the whole plant by gently tugging it from the ground. Larger beets may require a garden fork to gently loosen the surrounding soil before you pull them out.
Storage	To store, cut off the greens, leaving 2 to 3 inches of stem. The greens can be stored separately for up to a week in a plastic bag in the refrigerator. The roots can be placed in a plastic bag and will keep in the refrigerator for up to 3 weeks. If you have a large amount to store, they can be packed in a box filled with peat moss and stored in a root cellar.

Broccoli

Broccoli is a cool-season crop and is probably the easiest of all the brassica family to grow. Brassicas, also called cruciferous vegetables and known as the cabbage family, includes such favorites as broccoli, Brussels sprouts, cabbage, cauliflower, bok choy, and kale. They are cold-hardy vegetables that give you an exceptional harvest for the space they use. They grow well in most soil types. Adding shredded leaves to the area where you will be planting the following year will help to produce fabulous brassicas.

Most varieties of broccoli will produce one large head averaging about 6 to 8 inches in diameter. Once the head is harvested (usually with a small, sharp knife), the plant will continue to produce side branches with smaller heads. If you keep cutting these little heads before they flower, you can harvest broccoli from one plant for several weeks.

The broccoli plant will bolt when the weather gets hot. This means the plant will go to flower more quickly than it normally would in cooler weather. It is best to plant broccoli early in the spring (April) and then again in late summer for a fall harvest.

Broccoli often does best when transplanted. This allows you to start your plants indoors so they get more growth before the heat of the summer arrives.

Broccoli is one of the most popular vegetables for the health-conscious eater. A half cup of cooked broccoli has 75 mg vitamin C, 1,300 IU beta carotene, 3 grams protein, 5 grams dietary fiber, and only

40 calories, making it one of the most important foods in your garden and among the healthiest foods on your table.

QUICK TIPS FOR GROWING BROCCOLI	
Family name	Brassicaceae (mustard family).
Edible parts	Flower buds and stems.
Location	Cool area.
Best soil	Rich, moist but well-drained loamy soil; pH 6.0–6.8.
When to plant	Start indoors April to mid-July, then transplant out after 6 to 8 weeks.
How to plant	Space transplants 16 to 24 inches apart in rows spaced 2 to 3 feet apart. Sow seeds ½ inch deep, 4 inches apart, then thin seedlings to proper spacing.
How much to plant	10 to 15 plants per person each season.
Companion plants	For a positive effect, plant with beans, onions, potatoes, oregano, dill, sage, and nasturtiums. Planting with tomatoes and lettuce will have a negative effect on broccoli.
Watering	Water deeply at least once a week around the base of the plant. Hand-watering or drip irrigation are best. If an overhead sprinkler is used, the large leaves block the water from reaching the roots.
Fertilizing	Start to fertilize about 3 weeks after setting out the transplants and again when the bud starts to form on the plant.
Pests and diseases	Root maggots, cabbageworms, and club root are common. Crop rotation is essential to prevent pests and diseases.
When to harvest	Broccoli usually matures in 50 to 72 days. Cut the center head when it is about 5 to 6 inches in diameter or before the buds start to open.
How to harvest	Cut the center head with about 4 inches of stem using a sharp knife. The plant will form side branches off the main stem, which will produce smaller heads that need to be cut before they flower.
Storage	Broccoli will keep for a week or two in your refrigerator. To preserve its abundant nutrients, put your broccoli on ice or into the refrigerator as soon as it is harvested.

Brussels Sprouts

Brussels sprouts look like little palm trees with lumps growing from the plant stem, or trunk. The bumps, which are usually 1 to 2 inches in diameter, are the Brussels sprouts. They are often called "baby cabbages" because they look like miniature cabbages. Each plant should produce between 50 and 100 sprouts.

Brussels sprouts are a cool-season vegetable, usually planted in early spring or early fall because their taste is improved by a light frost. Like most other brassicas, these vegetables like to have a fertile, well-drained soil to grow in.

QUICK TIPS FOR GROWING BRUSSELS SPROUTS	
Family name	Brassicaceae (mustard family).
Edible parts	The sprouts, sometimes called the "bud."
Location	Cool area.
Best soil	Fertile, moist, well-drained soil; pH 6.0–6.8.
When to plant	Sow April to July and then transplant out in 6 to 8 weeks.
How to plant	Set out transplants 16 to 24 inches apart in rows spaced 2 to 3 feet apart. For direct seeding, sow seeds ½ inch deep and every 4 inches and then thin to 16 to 24 inches apart.
How much to plant	5 to 10 plants per person.
Companion plants	For a positive effect, plant with beans, beets, onions, potatoes, and oregano. Avoid planting near tomatoes, lettuce, and strawberries, as they may have a negative effect.
Watering	Water deeply at least once a week around the base of the plant. Hand-watering, a soaker hose, or drip irrigation are best. If an overhead sprinkler is used, the large leaves keep the water from reaching the roots.
Fertilizing	Start to fertilize about 3 weeks after setting out the transplants and again when the buds start to form on the plant.
Pests and diseases	Root maggots, cabbageworms, and club root are common. Crop rotation is essential for prevention of pests and diseases.
When to harvest	When the big leaves start to turn yellow, it is a sign that the sprouts are ready to be harvested, about 80-100 days from seed.

QUICK TIPS FOR GROWING BRUSSELS SPROUTS	
How to harvest	Harvest the sprouts from the bottom of the plant, moving upward until all the sprouts mature. The green sprouts should be 1 to 2 inches in diameter and will easily break off from the stem. Remove the bottom leaves as you harvest the sprouts.
Storage	Brussels sprouts can be kept for up to a week or so in the refrigerator. They can be frozen and used later.

Cabbage

Another easy-to-grow vegetable in the brassica family, cabbage is a cool-season crop that grows well in most soils. It is best to plant this vegetable in early spring for a summer harvest or in late summer for a fall harvest. The mature cabbage forms a head from a rosette of thickened leaves. The cabbage head can be round, pointy, or flattened depending on the variety. The leaves can be richly colored and textured. There are green varieties that produce light green leaves and red varieties with purplish red leaves. The Savoy cabbage has crinkly leaves. There are short-season and long-season varieties.

QUICK TIPS FOR GROWING CABBAGE	
Family name	Brassicaceae (mustard family).
Edible parts	Leaf heads.
Location	Cool area.
Best soil	Rich, moist but well-drained loamy soil; pH 6.0–6.8.
When to plant	Start indoors April to mid-July, then transplant out after 6 to 8 weeks.
How to plant	Space transplants 16 to 20 inches apart in rows 2 to 3 feet apart. Sow seeds ½ inch deep, 4 inches apart, then thin seedlings to proper spacing.
How much to plant	10 to 15 plants per person each season.
Companion plants	For a positive effect plant with beans, beets, onions, potatoes, and oregano. Planting with tomatoes and strawberries will have a negative effect on cabbage.

QUICK TIPS FOR GROWING CABBAGE	
Watering	Water deeply at least once a week around the base of the plant. Hand-watering and drip irrigation are best; if an overhead sprinkler is used, the large leaves block the water from reaching the roots.
Fertilizing	Start to fertilize about 3 weeks after setting out the transplants and again when the bud starts to form on the plant.
Pests and diseases	Root maggots, cabbageworms, and club root are common. Crop rotation is essential for prevention of pests and diseases.
When to harvest	Some varieties of cabbage will mature in 45 days; others can take several months to mature.
How to harvest	Cut the head of the cabbage off at the base of the plant using a sharp knife. The plant will form smaller heads if the roots of the plant have not been disturbed.
Storage	A head of a cabbage will last for a couple weeks in the refrigerator. If you live in a mild climate, the cabbage can be left out until you need it. Harvest before it gets large enough to split. Cabbage can be wrapped in newspaper, placed in boxes, and kept at 32 degrees over the winter. It can also be frozen and used as you need it.

Carrots

Carrots are among the most popular vegetables in the world. Pulling a baby carrot from the garden, wiping off the dirt, and biting into it is an experience not to be forgotten. There is nothing better than a freshly picked carrot! Carrots are great to grow if you have children around because they grow fairly quickly and can be picked at any size—and children love to pull them out of the ground.

Bed preparation is the time-consuming part of growing carrots. To grow their best, carrots need a deep, loose, sandy soil that is free of debris. They are excellent candidates for raised beds because the soil texture in them is often lighter than in a regular garden bed. If you have a heavy soil, it is important to dig in compost or aged animal manure to lighten the soil; however, if the soil is too fertile, the carrots may get hairy and misshapen and they may not taste as good. It can take a few years to get your soil to the proper consistency to grow fabulous carrots. If there are any obstructions in the soil, the carrot will grow around them, producing oddly shaped roots. It is important to take the time to break up any lumps of soil and pick out rocks that are larger than very small pebbles before planting your carrot seeds.

DOES EATING CARROTS REALLY HELP YOUR EYESIGHT?

Carrots are rich in phytonutrients called carotenoids, which are good for your eyesight, especially for seeing in poor light. It is best to eat carrots juiced or cooked because this makes the nutrients more available for the body to absorb.

Carrots are a cool-season crop and are best planted in the early spring to be harvested in the summer. If you live in an area where you get mild winters, plant another crop in late summer for a fall harvest. The carrot has its best flavor when grown in the full sun with cool nights. Carrots are direct seeded and need to be kept moist in order to germinate, so it may be necessary to water two to three times daily until they germinate. Water carefully so you don't wash the seeds away. It is important to keep the soil moistened because the seeds may not be able to break through the hard and crusty soil if it gets too dry.

QUICK TIPS FOR GROWING CARROTS	
Family name	Umbelliferae or Apiaceae (carrot, celery, or parsley family).
Edible parts	Roots.
Location	Sunny location.
Best soil	Fertile, sandy, loamy soil, free of debris; pH 5.5–6.8.
When to plant	Sow direct in April through mid-July. Plant a row every few weeks so you will be able to eat carrots all season long.
How to plant	Sow seeds ¼ inch deep, ½ inch apart, in rows spaced 12 to 24 inches apart. Seeds can take from 7 to 21 days to germinate and need to be kept moist until then. Once they are a few inches tall, thin them so plants are 2 to 4 inches apart.

QUICK TIPS FOR GROWING CARROTS	
How much to plant	25 to 30 feet per person each season.
Companion plants	For a positive effect, plant with beans, leeks, onions, peas, and radishes.
Watering	Water regularly, preferably with a drip irrigation system; carrots grow best if the leaves are not wet.
Fertilizing	Add compost or manure in the fall to the area where you will be growing your carrots the following spring.
Pests and diseases	Carrot flies, aphids, leafhoppers, and nematodes are some common pests that affect carrots.
When to harvest	Carrots will mature in 30 to 80 days, depending on whether you want to harvest baby carrots or fully mature ones. You can start harvesting carrots once they are about the size of your finger.
How to harvest	Gently pull the carrot out of the ground. For mature carrots, push them gently downward to break the roots, then pull them out. This will prevent them from breaking off underground.
Storage	When storing carrots, remove the tops. They will keep in a plastic bag in the refrigerator for several weeks, or they can be frozen or canned. If you have a large amount, leave them in the ground covered with several inches of mulch and harvest as you need them.

Cucumber

Cucumbers need to be pollinated, so it is important to know if the variety you choose is a hybrid or standard. Standard varieties have both male and female flowers on the same vine; insects or the wind will do the pollinating for you. The male flower comes out first and looks like a miniature cucumber. The female flower is identified by a swollen ovary just behind the male flower. Hybrid varieties have separate female and male plants and will need to be pollinated by hand using a Q-tip to transfer pollen from the flower to the ovary. If you have saved cucumber seeds from the past or a friend has given them to you and you are not sure of the variety, check the plant as it grows to see what kind of flowers it is producing. If there is only a male or female flower, no fruit will form. Go to your garden center and purchase seeds for another plant that will pollinate the first one for you.

QUICK TIPS FOR GROWING CUCUMBERS

Family name	Cucurbitaceae (gourd family).
Edible parts	Fruit.
Location	Cucumbers are great veggies for growing in greenhouses or containers.
Best soil	Rich, warm, well-drained, sandy soil; pH 5.5–6.8
When to plant	Plant in the spring once the soil temperature reaches 60°F.
How to plant	Can be direct seeded or transplanted. Sow seeds 1 inch deep, 6 inches apart, in rows 4 to 6 feet apart. This is the best way if you are trellising the cucumber plant.
How much to plant	5 to 20 feet per person depending on whether you are going to be pickling any of them.
Companion plants	Plant with beans, broccoli, cabbage, lettuce, peas, radishes, and tomatoes. Sage can have a negative effect on cucumber plants, so keep them apart.
Watering	Cucumbers need lots of water. Deep watering at the roots is better than using a sprinkler to reduce the risk of mildew, a fungus that grows in excess moisture on leaves. If the weather is warm, water the plants every second day, especially if they are growing in a greenhouse or container.
Care	Vining cucumbers are best grown on a trellis so the plant gets good air circulation and light. There are bush varieties as well. Pickle bush is one of my favorites for eating because the fruit stays small and sweet.
Fertilizing	Fertilize with manure tea or fish fertilizer 1 week after the plant blooms and then again 3 weeks later.
Pests and diseases	Aphids, cucumber beetles, flea beetles, mites, squash bugs, downy mildew, and powdery mildew can all affect the cucumber plant. Make sure you do not compost diseased plants!
When to harvest	Harvest the fruit when it is 6 to 12 inches long; this may vary depending on the variety. The cucumber will keep longer if harvested in the early morning, when it is cooler. Pick the fruit regularly so that new fruit will keep forming.
How to harvest	Cut the fruit from the plant rather than twisting or pulling it off, which can damage the plant.
Storage	Cucumbers will keep for up to one week in the refrigerator.

Garlic

Choose the biggest cloves to plant. The ones from the grocery are fine unless you are a connoisseur, in which case you can find endless varieties in garden catalogs. Mulch the beds after they are planted. Garlic will grow slowly over the winter and will shoot up quickly once the days start to get longer in January and February. In the spring, keep the plants well weeded and give them more mulch and regular watering if you do not get sufficient rain. In early spring, the garlic plants will produce flower stalks, which are called "scapes." These flowers can be eaten like garlic cloves. Removing the stem before it fully flowers will allow the plant to put more energy into producing a larger bulb.

The garlic bulbs are ready to be harvested once the garlic tops start to turn brown and die back. When harvesting garlic, use a garden fork to loosen the soil so the bulbs do not break off. Garlic needs to be dried in order for it to keep properly; leave the bulbs in the sun to cure for up to three weeks. Protect them from the rain by covering them or bringing them indoors in bad weather.

QUICK TIPS FOR GROWING GARLIC	
Family name	Alliaceae (onion family).
Edible parts	Bulb (cloves) and flower stem.
Location	Sunny, dry area.
Best soil	Rich, well drained; pH 6.0–6.8.
When to plant	Plant bulbs in the fall if you live in a warmer climate or in the early spring if you live in an extremely cold climate where the ground freezes in early fall.
How to plant	Set out cloves of garlic 2 inches deep, 6 to 8 inches apart in rows spaced 16 to 24 inches apart. Plant the cloves with the pointed end up.
How much to plant	5 to 10 feet per person.
Companion plants	For a positive effect, plant near carrots and tomatoes. Beans, peas, and strawberries can have a negative effect, so avoid planting them near garlic.
Watering	Needs regular watering in the spring if there is little rainfall.

QUICK TIPS FOR GROWING GARLIC	
Care	Mulch in the fall and again in the spring when the plants are 1 foot high to prevent weeds and keep the soil from drying out.
Fertilizing	Fertilize with compost tea or fish fertilizer after the flower stalks have started to form.
Pests and diseases	Aphids and thrips can be a problem. Using crop rotation will prevent most pests and disease.
When to harvest	Garlic takes 6 to 10 months to fully mature. When the tops start to turn brown and die back, garlic is ready to be harvested.
How to harvest	Loosen the soil around the plants with a garden fork and then gently pull out the bulbs, trying to keep the stem and bulb intact. The bulb will dry better if it is not broken off.
Storage	If dried and stored properly, garlic will keep for several months. Let bulbs cure in a sunny windowsill away from rain for a few weeks. Clean off any dirt remaining on the bulb and store it in a paper bag or box in a cool, dry storage area. Garlic can also be braided and hung in a cool, dark area.

Kale (also generally applies to collards, Swiss chard, and other leafy greens)

Kale has high levels of vitamin C and calcium and the highest levels of beta carotene of all the green vegetables. It is a hardy vegetable. Kale will survive over the winter and the leaves are more tender and sweet once they have been touched by frost. Kale will easily go to seed and spread throughout your garden, so pull the plants out before the seeds spread if you want to contain it.

There are several different varieties of kale, which are easily distinguishable because of their color and leaf. The most common are probably the green, curly leaf varieties.

QUICK TIPS FOR GROWING KALE

Family name	Brassicaceae (mustard family).
Edible parts	Leaves and stems.
Location	Cool, sunny area.
Best soil	Rich, well drained; pH 6.5–6.8.
When to plant	Start indoors April to mid-July, then transplant out after 6 to 8 weeks.
How to plant	Space transplants 18 to 20 inches apart in rows 2 to 3 feet apart. Sow seeds ¼ inch deep, 2 to 4 inches apart, then thin seedlings.
How much to plant	5 to 10 plants per person each season.
Companion plants	For a positive effect, plant with beans, onions, potatoes, dill, sage, and oregano. Planting with tomatoes and lettuce will have a negative effect on kale.
Weeding	Keep well weeded around the base of the plant.
Watering	Water deeply at least once a week around the base of the plant. Hand watering or drip irrigation are best; if an overhead sprinkler is used, the large leaves will block the water from the roots.
Fertilizing	Start to fertilize about 3 weeks after setting out the transplants and regularly until you harvest them.
Pests and diseases	Root maggots, cabbageworms, and club root are common. Crop rotation is essential for prevention of pests and disease.
When to harvest	Kale usually matures in 55 to 75 days.
How to harvest	Cut off leaves as you need them and the plant will keep producing for you all season long. Mature plants can be harvested at the base.
Storage	Eat the leaves as soon as possible after harvesting; they loose nutrients when stored. They will stay in the refrigerator for up to 1 week.

Lettuce

Lettuce is one of the most common vegetables for the home gardener, and it's very easy to grow. There are several types and varieties of lettuce you can choose to grow, including leaf lettuce, Bibb lettuce, romaine lettuce, and iceberg lettuce as well as the delightful mesclun mixes that contain arugula and other unusual greens and lettuces. With some leaf varieties, you can cut the outer leaves to eat, leaving the center to produce more new growth. You can also let the lettuce plant reach maturity and then cut the whole head at the base of the plant. Greens such as lettuce produce leaves quickly and are often harvested before the plant reaches maturity. They grow in various shades of greens and reds and have different flavors. Plan to plant several different varieties of lettuce in your garden so you can enjoy tasty and colorful salads. You want your salad stuff to grow rapidly for best flavor, so you'll need a rich soil high in nitrogen, and lots of water.

Lettuce is a cool-season vegetable and can be planted as soon as you can get into your garden. It grows great in containers on a patio or balcony as well. All types of lettuce have the same growing requirements. You want lettuce to grow rapidly for best flavor, so a nitrogen-rich soil is best. Nitrogen-rich fertilizer such as blood meal, alfalfa meal, composted horse manure, or aged chicken manure will help boost the nutrient content. Lettuce plants have quite shallow roots, so they are good candidates for the square foot bed. The soil should be moist, but well drained. Lettuce does not like soggy or saturated soil.

Lettuce has tiny seeds, so overseeding is probably one of the biggest problems in growing lettuce. If seeds are broadcasted (sowed over a wide area by hand), they will need to be thinned. One of the best ways to do this is to treat your garden bed as a transplant bed. As plants come up, gently move the seedlings to other areas of your garden or simply use your tender young thinnings in a salad.

Lettuce can be planted almost anywhere in your garden. It is a fast-growing vegetable, so you get quick results. To have lettuce all season long, start a few plants indoors in early spring. When you transplant those out to the garden, plant more seeds. Do this every few weeks. Lettuce is very heat sensitive, so you may find yourself without lettuce for a couple of weeks in the hottest part of summer. But that's not a major problem since at that time of year you have an abundance of tomatoes, peppers, squash, and cucumbers to fill in the nutritional gap. A great way to get the most out of your garden space is to plant some lettuce seeds or transplants under slower growing vegetables such as cabbage, cauliflower, and broccoli or even under a trellis where beans or cucumbers are growing. These larger plants will give the lettuce plants the shade they need during the summer months.

QUICK TIPS FOR GROWING LETTUCE	
Family name	Asteraceae (aster, daisy, or sunflower family).
Edible parts	Leaves and stems.
Location	Shady area with a cool temperature. Lettuce grows well in raised beds and containers.
Best soil	Loose, rich, well drained; pH 6.0–6.8.
When to Plant	For transplants, sow indoors early March to mid-July. Direct seed as soon as you can work your soil and plant more every few weeks for a steady supply.
How to plant	Can be transplanted or sown directly to the garden. Sow seeds ¼ inch deep, spacing them 8 to 10 inches apart in rows 12 to 24 inches apart.
How much to plant	20 to 25 plants per person each season.
Companion plants	For a positive effect, plant with beets, cabbage, peas, clover, and radish. There are no plants that have a negative effect on lettuce plants.
Watering	Drip irrigation or overhead sprinkling will work well. Plants need 1 to 2 inches each week and may require more if the weather is hot. Sprinkling the leaves in the early morning will help to keep the plant cooler during the hot part of the day.
Care	Provide some shade in the heat of the summer. A floating row cover works well.
Fertilizing	Add compost tea or fish fertilizer around the base of the plant every 2 to 3 weeks after planting.
Pests and diseases	Use crop rotation as prevention. Some common pests and diseases include slugs, aphids, cabbage loopers, flea beetles, downy mildew, and fusarium wilt.
When to harvest	Lettuce plants reach maturity at between 50 to 75 days. Harvest leaf and romaine lettuce when the plant is large enough to use. Harvest Bibb lettuce when a loose head is formed, and iceberg lettuce when the head is firm.
How to harvest	Cut or pull off leaves of leaf lettuce. For head lettuce varieties, use a sharp knife to cut off the heads at the base of the plant.

Onions

Anyone who cooks for a family knows that onions add flavor and vital nutrients to many dishes. Onions can be temperamental vegetables to grow. They like cool temperatures when they first start growing and then need heat in order to produce bulbs. They require a rich, clean (free of sticks or stones), well-drained soil. Onions are most commonly planted in the spring and harvested in the fall, but they can be planted in the fall and harvested early in the spring in areas with mild winters.

There are three ways of starting onions: by seed, with sets, or with transplants. Planting by seed is the slowest way; these need to be started as early as possible and they need 10 to 12 weeks to grow before they can be put into your garden. Sets are actually miniature, dormant onions that are raised for propagation. Sets planted in the spring will produce green onions within 3 or 4 weeks but will often bolt in warm weather before they produce a nice-sized bulb. If planted in the fall, they will be less likely to bolt in the cooler temperatures. Transplants are less likely than sets to bolt once the weather turns warm. You can grow your own transplants from seed or purchase them at a garden center in the spring.

Once the tops start to turn brown, the onions are nearing maturity. When the tops start to fall over, take a garden rake and gently bend all the browning tops over so all of them are lying down. Leave them this way for a few weeks and then start to pull onions as you need them. If the season is coming to an end and all of your onions need to be pulled, make sure you allow them to dry so they will store well.

QUICK TIPS FOR GROWING ONIONS	
Family name	Alliaceae (onion family).
Edible parts	Bulbs and leaves.
Location	Sunny area.
Best soil	Rich, moist but well-drained light soil, free of debris; pH 5.6–6.5.
When to plant	For summer harvest, start seeds in January or February for transplanting in the early spring, or place sets out in the spring. If you live in a mild climate, set out transplants or onion sets again in late summer for harvesting the following spring.

QUICK TIPS FOR GROWING ONIONS

How to plant	Sow seeds ½ inch deep in pots indoors. Plant sets or set out transplants 4 to 6 inches apart in rows spaced 16 to 24 inches apart.
How much to plant	30 to 60 feet per person if you want to store them.
Companion plants	For a positive effect, plant with beets, cabbage, carrots, lettuce, potatoes, and tomatoes. Beans and peas have a negative effect, so avoid planting them near your onions.
Watering	In the early stage of growth, onions need lots of water. Keep the soil moist. Stop watering once the leaves begin to turn brown.
Care	Onions like rich soil, so add several inches of compost or aged manure when preparing the garden bed.
Fertilizing	Side-dress with compost (place around the base of the plant) when the bulb first starts to swell and again when the leaves are about 1 foot tall.
Pests and diseases	Very few pests or diseases affect onions. Crop rotation is the best way to prevent possible problems.
When to harvest	Once the leaves have turned brown and died back, the bulbs are ready to be harvested. When growing sets for green onions, harvest once the greens are about 12 inches tall.
How to harvest	Gently loosen soil around the plant and then pull out the bulb.
Storage	Onions will store for several months if dried properly. Once the onions are harvested, lay them on a newspaper or a mesh screen in a sunny, dry area. Let them dry for seven to ten days, turning them few times each day. Make sure they are protected from any moisture or dampness.

Peppers

Peppers—whether bell peppers or any of a huge variety of hot and hotter peppers—are a little touchy to grow. They need lots of full sun, warm daytime temperatures, cool nighttime temperatures, fertile soil, and lots of water. Sweet peppers need a little less heat than hot pepper varieties. Peppers can be seeded directly if you have a long growing season; however, they often do better started indoors in early spring and transplanted out once the temperature reaches 65ºF.

Peppers are a very popular vegetable, either cooked by themselves or with other foods. They are also eaten raw in salads or as appetizers. When preparing to use your pepper, cut it in half, remove the stem, and rinse away the seeds. Fresh or dried hot peppers need to be handled carefully because the oils in the skin can burn your skin or eyes. It is suggested that you use rubber gloves and hold the hot pepper under water when preparing it. Remove the seeds from a hot pepper if you want to cut down the heat; the seeds add to the hot taste.

QUICK TIPS FOR GROWING PEPPERS

Family name	Solanaceae (nightshade family).
Edible parts	Fruits.
Location	Very sunny area.
Best soil	Fertile, well-drained soil that does not have an excess of nitrogen; soil that is too rich will form leaves but not much fruit; pH 5.5–6.8.
When to plant	Sow seeds indoors 8 to 10 weeks before you plan to put them into your garden. Transplant them when the daytime temperature is 65°F.
How to plant	Set out plants 18 inches apart in rows spaced 30 to 36 inches apart.
How much to plant	5 to 10 plants per person.
Companion plants	Plant with basil, carrots, onions, oregano, and marjoram. Fennel will have a negative effect on peppers, so avoid planting them near each other.
Watering	Water regularly and keep soil moist when the plant is flowering and fruiting.
Fertilizing	Use fish fertilizer or compost tea after the first bloom and then after the fruit starts to form.
Pests and diseases	Aphids, armyworms, Colorado potato beetles, corn borers, mites, and cutworms are some common pests.
When to harvest	Peppers mature between 60 and 95 days after planting depending on the variety. Harvest sweet peppers when they are firm and full-sized. You can harvest them when they are green or leave them to turn red, orange, or yellow, depending on the variety. Harvest hot peppers when they are full-sized and have turned yellow, red, or dark green, again depending on the variety.
How to harvest	Cut or gently pull the pepper from the plant, leaving a stem of ½ inch.
Storage	Fresh peppers will last 1 to 2 weeks in the refrigerator if not washed and placed in a sealed plastic bag. Peppers can be frozen, dried, and preserved by pickling or canning them.

Potatoes

Potatoes are the most commonly used vegetable in the world. They are nutritious, versatile, easy to grow, and ideal for storage. Potatoes are closely related to tomatoes and like tomatoes, they produce sprawling and bushy vines above ground. However, potatoes produce tubers underground. They need a long growing season—approximately four months with continuous cool weather—for best production. When preparing the potato bed, make sure the soil is well tilled with compost or aged manure added to it. Potatoes need a more acidic soil than most vegetables do, so never lime in the area where they will be planted.

Potatoes should be planted as early as you can get into your garden. They are grown from seed potatoes, each one cut into pieces containing 2 or 3 eyes. Let the cut pieces callus over (become dry on the surface) in a well-aerated location like your kitchen counter for a few days so they won't rot when you put them into the ground. A potato plant can take up a lot of room and several plants will be needed for a small family to eat them fresh. You'll want even more if you want to store them for using during the winter months.

The potato does not need much water until it has sprouted above ground. After the vine starts to grow, keep mounding soil up against the new growth. This process is called "hilling." This allows the tuber to grow without being exposed to the sun; too much sun exposure will cause potatoes to turn green. You can harvest young potatoes after the plant has flowered by digging around the base of the plant with your hands.

QUICK TIPS FOR GROWING POTATOES	
Family name	Solanaceae (nightshade family).
Edible parts	Tubers.
Location	Sunny area.
Best soil	Fertile, slightly acidic, sandy loam soil, moist but well drained; pH 4.8–6.0.
When to plant	Seed them as soon as you can work your garden bed in the spring; potatoes thrive in cool weather.
How to plant	Cut seed potatoes into pieces, making sure each piece has at least 2 eyes. Plant 4 inches deep, 12 to 16 inches apart, in rows spaced 36 to 48 inches apart.

QUICK TIPS FOR GROWING POTATOES

How much to plant	10 to 30 row feet per person.
Companion plants	For positive effects, plant with beans, cabbage, corn, lettuce, onions, marigolds, and radish. Do not plant near pumpkins or tomatoes, both of which can have a negative effect on your potato plants.
Watering	Water regularly from the time the vine first emerges aboveground until the plant flowers. After flowering, the plant needs less water, and rainfall is usually sufficient if the plants are mulched.
Care	Keep mounding up (hilling) soil around the vine as it grows; this helps to keep the potatoes covered.
Fertilizing	Fertilize with compost tea once the flowers start to emerge.
Pests and diseases	Wireworms, Colorado beetles, scab, aphids, and flea beetles are some common pests and diseases.
When to harvest	Potatoes mature 90 to 120 days after being planted. New or small potatoes can be harvested once the plant has flowered. When the vine turns brown and dies back, the tubers are fully mature and can be stored for longer periods.
How to harvest	Harvest in the morning when the temperature is cool. For new potatoes, you can just dig around under the vine and pull out a few potatoes for your dinner. Once the vine has died back, pull the vine and gently dig the larger tubers with a garden fork.
Storage	Potatoes are a great vegetable for storing and will keep for several months if stored properly. Make sure they are dry before storing them in a cool, dark area. If you have the space, such as in a big open cellar or insulated shed, spread them in a single layer on newspapers or in a ventilated box.

Spinach

Spinach is a cool-season crop that does best grown in spring or fall when the temperatures are lower and the days are shorter. Spinach has one of the darkest colored leaves and is one of the richest sources of vitamin and minerals in your garden.

Some common varieties for planting in spring and fall are Tyee and Olympia. For summer planting, try New Zealand spinach, a trailing perennial plant that produces thicker leaves. It does well in mild climates.

Spinach is easy to grow, but it bolts easily in warm weather, so it is best grown either early or late in the season. When a vegetable "bolts" it means it has grown too quickly and starts to produce seeds. The taste and flavor of the spinach is compromised once it begins to bolt. It needs a rich soil, so prepare your garden bed with several inches of compost or aged animal manure.

Spinach does best in full sun, which is one of the reasons it is best grown early or late in the season when the sun is not too hot. Make sure the garden bed is well drained, especially if you live in a wet climate.

QUICK TIPS FOR GROWING SPINACH

Family name	Chenopodiaceae (goosefoot family).
Edible parts	Leaves and stems.
Location	Full sun.
Best soil	Rich soil abundant in nitrogen; pH 6.2–6.9.
When to plant	Cool weather, early spring and early fall. Start sowing indoors in April to July and transplant out every 4 weeks, or direct seed as soon as the soil is worked.
How to plant	Can be direct seeded or transplanted. Plant seeds ½ inch deep, 1 inch apart; space plants 6 to 8 inches apart in rows at least 12 inches apart.
How much to plant	10–15 plants per person each season.
Companion plants	For a positive effect, plant with cabbage, celery, eggplants, onions, peas, and strawberries. There are no plants that have a negative effect on spinach.
Watering	Keep soil moist; sprinkling will keep the leaves cooler in warm weather.
Care	May need a little shade if the weather gets warm. A floating row cover works well.
Fertilizing	Give spinach plants a nitrogen-rich fertilizer once they are one-third grown, or approximately once every 10 to 14 days.
Pests and diseases	Aphids, slugs, cabbageworms, and leaf miners are common.
When to harvest	Can be harvested at any size from baby leaves to maturity, which ranges from 40 to 50 days.
How to harvest	Cut outer leaves as they grow or at the base of a mature plant.
Storage	Spinach does not store well. Wash leaves, dry them in a salad spinner, and place them in a sealed plastic bag or container. Spinach will keep in the refrigerator for a few days. Lightly steamed spinach can easily be frozen.

Squash (includes pumpkins, pumpkin seeds, winter squashes, zucchini, and summer squash)

Squash is an easy vegetable to grow, and each plant can produce a large number of fruits. There are two types of squash—summer and winter. The main differences between these are the amount of time they take to mature and how well they will store once harvested. Summer squash is a warm-weather vegetable that is eaten before the fruit has fully matured. The skin and seeds are eaten as part of the whole fruit. The winter squash takes longer to mature and are usually harvested in the late summer or fall. They usually have a larger fruit than summer varieties and the skin is tough and inedible. The seeds are often removed before cooking as well. Some varieties, such as pumpkin, produce lovely edible seeds that have very high nutritional value and can be eaten raw after removing from the hulls using the same technique as used for sunflower seeds. Flowers of all types of squash are edible and add delicate flavors to soups and salads.

Squash likes a rich soil that has plenty of organic matter. They often grow best in the compost pile! They are a vine vegetable that can spread six to eight feet across, so make sure you give them lots of room when planning your garden layout. Squash can be direct seeded or put out as transplants, which is usually dependent on the length of your growing season. Each plant—especially the summer zucchini squash—can produce lots of fruit seemingly overnight, so a plant or two is usually enough for any family. Winter squash can also produce several fruits from one plant, but if cured properly they will store for several months so you can enjoy them over time. Squash plants require lots of water. Since the leaves become very large, it is best to water the plant by hand or with drip irrigation around the base of the plant so the water reaches the roots. Squash leaves are more susceptible to mildew if they get wet.

QUICK TIPS FOR GROWING SQUASH

Family name	Cucurbitaceae (gourd family).
Edible parts	Fruits and some seeds.
Location	Sunny area.
Best soil	Fertile, well-drained, light soil. If you have clay soil, add lots of organic matter to lighten it; pH 5.5–6.8.
When to plant	Sow seeds directly when the soil temperature is 60°F. You can start transplants in April and transplant them out approximately 6 weeks later, making sure the soil temperature is warm enough.
How to plant	Sow seeds 2 to 3 inches deep, 16 inches apart in rows 3 to 5 feet apart.
How much to plant	For summer squash, plant 1 to 2 plants for the family. For winter squash, plant 4 to 10 plants per family.
Companion plants	Plant with beans, corn, radishes, mint, and nasturtiums. Potatoes can have a negative effect, especially on summer squash varieties, so avoid planting them near each other.
Weeding	Keep well weeded when the plant is young.
Watering	Squash requires regular watering. Watering at the base of the plant rather than overhead is better for the plant.
Care	Plants need a large amount of space to grow.
Fertilizing	Give the plants fish fertilizer or compost tea once they have reached about 1 foot tall and are just starting to spread.
Pests and diseases	Aphids, cucumber beetles, mites, nematodes, squash bugs, squash vine borers, and powdery mildew can affect squash plants.
When to harvest	Summer squash will mature in 50 to 65 days. Winter squash takes 60 to 110 days to grow to maturity. For summer squash, harvest once fruits start to form and pick every few days when the fruit is still fairly small (6 to 8 inches); they are tastier when young. For winter squash, harvest when the skin is hard. Gently use your fingernail to pierce the skin. If it leaves a mark, it is not ready to be harvested; if there is no mark, it is ready for harvesting.
How to harvest	Cut from the plant, leaving a small stem on each fruit.
Storage	Summer squash will store for up to 1 week in the refrigerator. If cured properly, winter squash will store for several months. Cure winter varieties by leaving the cut fruit in the sun for several days. Turn the fruit every few hours so all sides will be exposed to the sun. Cover them if they will be left out at night.

Strawberries

Strawberries belong in a category of their own when it comes to growing plants. I love them . . . and so do birds, so prepare to protect your berries with netting if you want any left for your own table.

You can easily grow strawberries in containers. A small garden patch in the full sun will give you a good yield. If you select June-bearing plants (the most popular because of their large, sweet fruit), you can expect many runners. Prune off all but 10 percent of the runners for the strongest plants and best yields. Everbearing and day-neutral strawberries will bear more than once a year and have few runners, but the fruit is smaller and not as sweet. Most strawberries are perennials, but a few varieties are biennials and will need to be replaced every other year. Once you have established a good strawberry bed, it will last for several years. During the first year, pinch off all the blossoms. You wont get any fruit, but you'll get strong heavy-bearing plants for years to come.

To avoid fungal diseases common in plants from the nightshade family, do not plant your vulnerable strawberries where tomatoes, potatoes, peppers, or eggplants have been grown in the past two years.

QUICK TIPS FOR GROWING STRAWBERRIES	
Family name	Fragaria.
Edible parts	Fruit and leaves.
Location	Full sun.
Best soil	Rich, loamy, well-drained soil; pH 5.8–6.2
When to plant	Plant in spring as soon as soil is dry enough to be worked or in late fall.
How to plant	Make a little mound in your hole for the crown and spread the roots out on the mound, then cover with soil. Most people buy strawberry plants, and most often they are propagated by runners. It is possible to grow them from seed. Plants started from seed in the spring will start producing fruit in their second year. Pinch off the first year's flower to insure strong root growth. Set plants 18 inches apart in rows 4 to 4 ½ feet apart because of their spreading habit. You can root runners by placing them in a row next to the mother plants, anchors with a rock or ½ inch of soil. Do not sever runners from the mother plant.

QUICK TIPS FOR GROWING STRAWBERRIES	
How much to plant	10 to 15 plants per person.
Companion plants	Bush beans, lettuce, onions, spinach. Avoid planting near cabbage.
Watering	1-2 inches of water per week is needed for juicy fruit. Water is especially important during fruit formation period.
Fertilizing	Use a 10-10-10 fertilizer , one pound per 100 square feet. Do not fertilize late in the season.
Pests and diseases	Vertilicillium wilt, botrytis, rood rot. Choose resistant varieties, be sure to rotate crops.
When to harvest	Wait until they are fully ripened on the plant for the juiciest fruit. It's best when the fruit seems to be ready to fall off the plant.
How to harvest	Gently pinch the stem above the berry rather than pulling on the berry.
Storage	Strawberries will keep for a few days in the refrigerator. There can easily be frozen. A popular means of preserving them is to make them into jams and jellies.

Swiss Chard

Like most other greens, Swiss chard likes a well-drained, nitrogen-rich soil. Start planting in early spring. As you harvest the outer stems, the plant will keep producing more. A few plants will take you all the way through several weeks of harvesting.

Swiss chard is a power food with many of the main nutrients for healing and overall health. Tiny leaves can be eaten raw in a salad, but as the plant grows, the best way to maximize the nutrients in Swiss chard is to steam it for two to three minutes. A quick steaming will retain the bright color of this vegetable as well.

Swiss chard is one of the most colorful vegetables. It comes in a rainbow of colors—red, yellow, orange, green, and white. Common varieties include Fordhook Giant, Rhubarb, Canary Yellow, and Perpetual.

QUICK TIPS FOR GROWING SWISS CHARD

Family name	Chenopodiaceae (goosefoot family).
Edible parts	Leaves and stems.
Location	Sunny area.
Best soil	Rich, loamy, well-drained soil; pH 6.5–6.8.
When to plant	Sow indoors in March or April and transplant out in 4 weeks or direct seed as soon as your soil is worked.
How to plant	Can be directed seeded or transplanted. Sow seeds ½ inch deep, 1 to 2 inches apart, in rows spaced at least 18 inches apart. Thin plants so they are 8 to 12 inches apart.
How much to plant	10 to 15 plants per person each season.
Companion plants	Plant with cabbage, celery, eggplants, onions, peas, and strawberries for a positive effect. There are no plants that have a negative effect on Swiss chard.
Watering	Keep soil moist. Drip irrigation or hand-watering are recommended over sprinkling. As the leaves get larger they will impede overhead watering from reaching the plant roots.
Fertilizing	Use a nitrogen-rich fertilizer 2 to 3 weeks after transplanting or when the plants reach about 6 inches high.
Pests and diseases	Use crop rotation as prevention. Beware of cabbageworms, aphids, flea beetles, and leaf spot.
When to harvest	Plants mature in 45 to 50 days. Outer leaves can be eaten at any size; baby leaves are often used in salads.
How to harvest	Break off the outer leaves or cut them with a sharp knife.
Storage	Swiss chard will not store long. Wash leaves and dry them in a salad spinner. For the optimal nutrients, it's best to harvest what you're going to eat immediately, but you can place the greens in a sealed plastic bag or container and keep them in the refrigerator for a few days.

Tomatoes

A ripe tomato just picked off the vine is heaven on earth! Tomatoes are the most popular vegetables eaten in North America and most gardeners, like me, count them as the number one reason they garden. If you think of a tomato being round and red, think again. There are varieties that produce yellow, orange, and even purple fruit and others that produce a fruit that is pear- or plum-shaped. The size of the tomato can range from 1 to 6 inches in diameter, depending on the variety you choose. One plant will produce an abundance of fruit for you to enjoy.

Tomatoes will grow well in any backyard as long as it is sunny and hot. They do well in containers and in greenhouses, especially if you live in a cooler climate. I keep a couple of very prolific cherry tomato plants in containers on my deck for super-easy snacking.

Tomato seeds are best started indoors, where you can regulate the temperature so they will germinate. Tomato seedlings need 6 to 8 weeks of growth before they are ready to be transplanted into the garden or a container. Introduce the plant to the cool outdoors gradually over several days when you are ready to transplant your tomato plants, a process called "hardening off."

Unlike most plants, tomato plants like to be planted deep. Remove the lower leaves and bury at least half of the stem underground to give the plant a strong root base. Tomatoes need supports so the stem won't break under the weight of the fruit. A simple tomato cage keeps the fruit from touching the ground and allows air circulation around the plant.

Gardeners often give tomato plants either too much or too little water. When you first transplant a tomato plant, water it every few days until it is well established. Once the plant reaches 2 to 3 feet tall, the roots are probably just as deep; a little water each day will not reach where the roots need it the most. Tomatoes need a deep watering once a week or every 10 days. If your fruit starts to split, the plant is not getting enough water or it is getting too much water.

If you are planning to grow your tomato plants in containers, it is best to choose dwarf or hanging varieties unless you have a very large container. A standard tomato needs a container at least 18 inches deep.

ORGANIC PEST SPRAY

Cayenne pepper and garlic spray will go a long way toward keeping cabbage moths and other pests away from your plants. Make this natural pesticide by throwing a bulb of garlic (it's not necessary to peel it), 2 tablespoons of cayenne pepper, and about a quart of water into your blender. Process for about a minute then strain it through a piece of cheesecloth. Add 3-4 drops of dish detergent to help it stick and pour it into a spray bottle. When you spray it on your plants, it will not only keep insects away, it'll clear your sinuses as you spray! Be careful not to get it into your eyes.

QUICK TIPS FOR GROWING TOMATOES

Family name	Solanaceae (nightshade family).
Edible parts	Fruit.
Location	Sunny and warm area.
Best soil	Fertile, well drained; pH 5.5–6.8.
When to plant	Sow seeds early in spring; it can take 6 to 8 weeks before they are ready to go into the garden bed. Make sure the daytime temperature is 65°F before you put them outside and you've passed your frost-free date.
How to plant	Set out transplants 12 to 18 inches apart in rows spaced 36 to 48 inches apart. Bury at least half of the stem underground when setting them out, pinching off any leaves that will be underground.
How much to plant	10 to 20 plants per person, depending on whether you want to can or preserve any fruit.
Companion plants	Plant with asparagus, basil, cabbage, carrot, onion, parsley, peas, and sage. Potatoes and fennel can have a negative effect, so avoiding planting them near each tomatoes.
Watering	Water deeply once a week or every 10 days when the weather is hot.

QUICK TIPS FOR GROWING TOMATOES

Care	In cooler climates, tomatoes may need protection to grow their best. In the Pacific Northwest, the rain is also a concern because tomato plants do not like their leaves to get wet. In this climate, consider growing them under a plastic or glass shelter. If the temperature reaches above 100°F, tomato plants will stop producing fruit, so make sure there is good ventilation if you grow tomatoes under shelter.
Fertilizing	Fertilize with fish fertilizer or compost tea 2 weeks before and again 2 weeks after the first picking.
Pests and diseases	Aphids, cutworms, tomato hornworms, flea beetles, leaf miners, nematodes, whiteflies, fusarium wilt, verticillium wilt (also known as early and late blight), tobacco mosaic, and blossom end rot can all affect your tomato plants. Some hybrid varieties are resistant to certain diseases and others are more resistant to other diseases, so check to see what disease are most common in your area and keep that in mind when you're deciding which varieties to plant.
When to harvest	Most varieties will mature 50 to 90 days after they have been transplanted into the garden or container.
How to harvest	Gently pluck the tomato from the vine.
Storage	A ripe tomato will keep for up to 1 week on your kitchen counter. Tomatoes do not ripen well in the refrigerator. Before first frost, you may still have lots of green tomatoes. Harvest, wrap them in newspaper, and place them in a cardboard box in a warm room. Check them regularly, pulling them out when they have ripened and discarding any that are beginning to rot. Tomatoes can be frozen whole or chopped. They also can be canned whole or diced, or made into sauces, salsa, or chutney to be enjoyed all winter.

CHAPTER 6

Growing Your Herbs

Herbs are wonderful medicinals, as you discovered in Chapter 2, and they can also spice up your life by adding delightful flavors to your favorite foods. You can grow herbs indoors or outdoors because, with few exceptions, most herbs are small and compact.

Technically, an herb is a perennial woody-stemmed plant with upper parts that die back to the roots in winter. That definition would include rosemary, sage, lavender, oregano, thyme, mint, and many other favorites. But it would exclude basil and dill and cilantro. What would life be without these delicious medicinals?

The main thing to remember about herbs is that many of them are Mediterranean in origin, so think arid climates, lots of sun, and few nutrients. Still, there are woodland herbs, and there are some, like mints, that will not only thrive, but take over anywhere you plant them.

I've never regretted the day I tilled up my entire front yard and planted it in herbs. Most of the residents of my front-yard garden really require little attention. In fact, the most attention I give my oregano is to give it a serious haircut a couple of times a year to prevent it from sprawling all over the other plants. I mercilessly jerk out several kinds of mints, thoughtlessly planted years ago with undeserved affection and now the bane of my other herbs. From this 15' x 15' herbal wonderland, I harvest many of our medicinal needs as well as flavorings for the kitchen.

If you don't have the space or inclination to have an herb garden of that size, not to worry. One of the best things about herbs is that you can grow a plant or two here and there in your landscape (many are beautiful and make good ornamentals) or in a pot on your windowsill. Herbs can also help keep away insect pests in your vegetable garden, so it's always helpful to have several basil plants and perhaps some mints (in pots) near your veggies.

Also among the many delights of herb gardening is the fragrance of your crops and their ability to attract butterflies. Your herb garden will give you pleasure and health for years to come.

Basic gardening rules apply equally to herbs, with the few important additions that follow.

Sun

Most herbs need six to eight hours of direct sunlight daily for optimal growth and production of the volatile oils that give them their medicinal properties. A few herbs, like angelica, woodruff, and sweet cicely, like partial shade.

Soil

Regular garden soil works well for your herb plants. It should be as close to neutral pH as possible, between 6.5 and 7.0. Think back to the Mediterranean origins of our most beloved herbs and the generally poor soil quality found there. That's where these plants thrive. If your soil is too rich, you'll get growth but few volatile oils and less flavor. Herbs do need nourishment, but not much more than they'd get from a couple of trowelsful of compost dug in around them once a year.

Your soils must be well drained. Herbs hate wet feet! If you're not sure about drainage, try this easy "perk" test:

- Dig a hole about 8 inches deep and wide.
- Fill it with water.
- If it takes more than ten minutes for the water to drain out, you'll need to locate your herb garden somewhere else or install some drainage tiles in the area.

Preparing Your Herb Garden Site

If this is a first-time planting, dig down about 15 inches and turn and loosen the soil. If there is little topsoil, add organic matter like shredded leaves and compost to improve soil quality. Remove all stones and roots.

Plant. Water. Enjoy! If you've bought full-grown plants, you have instant herbs that you can snip and harvest spring, summer, and fall.

How to Grow Perennial Herbs

Most perennial herbs grow best from cuttings that show a small amount of root growth at the nodes. You can also buy plants from your closest nursery. Annual herbs are easily grown from seed, and some will self-sow for years of yield from one seed packet.

A word of caution about members of the mint family: A whole new forest of mint plants can grow from a 1-inch section of root, so once it is in your garden, it is nearly impossible to remove it. I planted a whole variety of mints in my herb garden when I first established it and now, twelve years later, it's a weekly struggle to keep them from taking over everything else. The best way to restrain mints is to plant them in a pot sunk into the ground and snip off any runners that escape.

If you want any of the members of the mint family in your garden, surely a fellow gardener will be more than happy to give you cuttings.

Chamomile (Matricaria recutita): Everyone needs to have a chamomile patch—even if it is in a pot—since chamomile is so useful for so many conditions. There are several varieties of chamomile, some growing as high as 30 inches. All have daisylike flowers with feathery fennel-like leaves. The most common ones are low-growing ground covers that like full sun and a little richer, moister soil than some of the Mediterranean herbs prefer. German chamomile, the most often used medicinal, is an annual that grows easily from seed sown directly in the garden after all danger of frost has passed. In warm climates, chamomile can be evergreen. It will often self-seed, and your bed, once established, will continue indefinitely.

Fennel *(Foeniculum vulgare)*: Prized for its seeds and beautiful feathery foliage, fennel is one of the most useful herbs in your garden. The plant can grow as high as 6 feet and spread 3 feet wide, so give it plenty of room. It likes full sun and grows best in slightly enriched soil. Fennel is easy to grow; in fact, it can drop seed everywhere, so you may have to pull out those unwanted volunteer plants.

Horehound *(Marrubiam vulgare)*: This member of the mint family (all mints are easily identifiable by their square stems) has attractive crinkled, hairy, wooly leaves and can thrive in the poorest of soils. It doesn't do well when fertilized. It reaches a maximum of 30 inches high and 12 inches wide. Like other members of the mint family, it can become invasive if it's not restrained.

Lavender *(Lavandula angustifolia)*: This fragrant annual is a beautiful addition to your herb garden. The most common English lavenders are hardy to zone 5 and love sun, heat, and dry soil. They will not tolerate high humidity or poor drainage. Despite their sun-loving natures, English lavenders are able to withstand cold northern winters. The only real trick to growing lavender is that you need to prune the leafy stems back by about one-third as soon as the plant finishes blooming for maximum plant strength.

Oregano *(Origanum vulgare)*: Another member of the sprawling mint family, oregano has a tendency to take over your garden, as I've learned the hard way. If you grow it in a pot sunk into the ground, you'll have less sprawl to cope with. It loves full sun and well-drained soil, but it's not persnickety about high-quality soil. Dividing clumps every two to three years will improve the intensity of the volatile oils and the medicinal quality and flavor.

Peppermint *(Mentha piperita)*: Peppermint, one our most valuable medicinals, comes in a wide variety of flavors, including my favorites, chocolate and apple. It is the most aggressively invasive of all the mints, so plant it in a sunken pot and give it frequent haircuts.

Although peppermint is sun-loving, it will do well in partial shade and may be slightly less invasive with a little less sun. Unlike many of its cousins, peppermint likes rich, moist soil.

Rosemary *(Rosmarinus officinalis)*: There's nothing quite like the refreshing scent of rosemary. In some parts of the country, it grows like a shrub and people take hedge trimmers to it. In our zone 7, it seems to last two or three winters before succumbing to the cold. I've even devised heat sinks, little stone walls around the plants to hold the winter sun's warmth, with only limited success. In most parts of the country, it's probably best to grow rosemary in a pot and bring it inside or keep it in a greenhouse in winter. Be aware that rosemary is very susceptible to several types of fungus and needs good air circulation, especially in winter. It needs full sun and prefers sandy soil.

Sage *(Salvia officinalis)*: Think desert when you are planting your sage. It loves dry, sandy soil and lots of sun. There are hundreds of varieties, most of which grow about 2 feet high with leaves of a distinctive gray-green color. If you live above zone 5, you'll probably want to bring your plants in for winter.

Thyme *(Thymus vulgaris)*: Thyme is available in hundreds of varieties, most of which are low growing and make good ground covers. I love my lemon-scented thyme, and so does my dog. He "swims" in it to perfume himself. It could be a lot worse. Like rosemary, thyme loves dry, sandy, well-drained soil and lots of sun. If it gets too wet, the roots will rot.

How to Grow Annual Herbs

All of our annual herbs are easily grown from seed sown directly into the soil. Since most of these annual herbs are not at all frost tolerant, you might want to keep a few plants indoors for the winter. In my mind, dried basil and cilantro are nearly tasteless and not worth the trouble, although I have successfully frozen both herbs in water in ice cube trays to keep their flavor nearly intact.

Basil *(Ocimum basilicum)*: Garden centers offer a wide variety of basil in varying intensities of color and flavor, including my favorite, purple basil. It needs full sun and a fairly rich soil, so it will be happy with a little extra compost. Keep the flowers pinched back for better leaf growth. The more individual leaves you harvest, the more growth you will get, so freely pinch what you want for meals.

Cilantro *(Coriandrum sativum)*: Since cilantro quickly cycles through its life span of pungent cilantro leaves and goes to seed called coriander, plant it at about three-week intervals throughout the season to keep a steady supply. It will self-seed freely as soon as soil temperatures reach 75°F. In the heat of summer, your plants may bolt very quickly. Cilantro is one of the few herbs that can tolerate a little shade, so morning sun and afternoon shade would be a perfect mix.

Dill *(Anethum graveolens)*: Dill can easily be sown straight into the garden soil in spring and enjoyed all season along. The fern-like leaves, called dill weed, can be harvested and eaten, with the younger leaves being the most flavorful. At the end of the season, the leaves and seeds can be harvested and dried. Dill likes full sun and a well-drained soil.

How to Harvest Herbs

Most perennial herbs are harvested when they develop flower buds, which is when their volatile oils reach the greatest intensity. It's best to pick your herbs in the early morning when their fragrance—hence their volatile oils—is at its peak. You can give them a light spray of water to remove any dust, pick off any yellowed or insect-laced leaves, and you're ready to go.

Basil, which is an annual, should be pinched back to prevent it from flowering. This encourages more leaf growth. Basil leaves can be harvested throughout the season as you like, but it's very cold sensitive, so before first frost, harvest all you have and dry it or make pesto and freeze.

Cilantro is also an annual, but it wildly self-seeds, so once you have cilantro, you're likely to keep having it indefinitely. Its incarnation as a leafy herb is relatively short-lived, so grab it when the leaves are hand-shaped, since it will soon morph into coriander. The coriander seeds are delicious but not as universally used as cilantro.

If you're harvesting seeds from coriander or any other seed you want to save, be sure to wait for them to fully ripen. Then carefully snip the seed head into a paper bag and leave the loosely packed bag open for several days in a sunny spot to ensure the seeds are dry.

Preserving Your Herb Harvest

Air-drying is the best and easiest way to preserve herbs. I have a "high-tech" herb dryer inside my front porch that consists of a string wrapped around nails pounded around the inside edge of the ceiling. You can simply hang loosely tied bundles, heads down (be sure to label them—you'll be surprised how all herbs look alike when they are dried), and let them air-dry for a few days before storing them in labeled glass jars in your herb cabinet. The essential elements for drying herbs are air circulation and keeping them from rain.

For very small-leafed herbs, simply sandwich them between a couple of old screens and prop them up on some bricks or cinder blocks to keep them off the ground. Do this on a sunny summer day, morning to night, and your herbs will be dry before sunset.

Be sure your herbs are completely dry before you store them or they will mold. When you're ready to use your herbs, check them carefully for mold. If you find any mold, do not use them; the mold could be harmful. If you store your herbs in glass jars and keep them away from the light, you'll help preserve their potency.

Tinctures

Many herbs can be successfully made into medicinal tinctures that will remain potent for years. Echinacea, valerian root, and feverfew leaves are just a few popular herbs that can be made into tinctures.

The tincture process is quite simple:

1. Harvest your material (leaves, flowers, or roots) early in the day when the plant is just beginning to bloom, usually about mid-summer. For root material, you can carefully dig up the plant, remove an inch or two of the main root, and replant it without harm to the plant.
2. Wash the materials carefully, paying special attention to clean all dirt off any roots you are using.
3. Sterilize your canning jars and lids dipping them briefly in boiling water, holding them with tongs.
4. Pack plant material loosely in a sterilized glass canning jar.
5. Cover the plant material completely with 100-proof vodka. Alternatively, if you prefer not to have alcohol-based tinctures, you can use vinegar, but the tincture will only last a year or two as compared to an alcohol-based tincture that may last as long as ten years.
6. Put the lid on the jar and store it in a dark place for about six weeks. After that time, the volatile oils from your herb will have infused the medium (either vodka or vinegar) and your tincture will be usable.
7. Using a cheesecloth and a funnel, decant your tincture into smaller bottles. I recommend dropper bottles as they can help you accurately measure the amount you're using. Label the bottles carefully, and compost the plant material that remains. Don't use your hands to squeeze the moisture from the plant material, since you can absorb it through your skin. (If you're working with valerian, you might very well find yourself dozing off in the middle of tincture-making!)

Note: Since it is impossible for the home herbalist to determine the strength of these preparations and since it will vary wildly, it's difficult to determine how much you need to take to get results. Results will also vary among individuals, so you will want to keep a journal of what you used, what batch, and the results. For example, if you're having difficulty sleeping, you can take valerian tincture and start with about five drops. If you don't get success with that, increase it to maybe seven or eight drops until you get results. Once you determine how much you need, you can add your personal dosage to the label.

Salves

Salves are carriers for medicinals you apply to your skin. The essence of the plant material is extracted in oils, which is then added to beeswax to make a salve. I've very successfully made comfrey, chamomile, and oregano salves that we use for our entire family, including all our critters.

Here's the process: Follow the steps used to make a tincture, but except for covering your plant material with alcohol or vinegar, cover with extra-virgin olive oil and add one capsule of vitamin E per quart to prevent spoilage. After six weeks, you are ready to use the extracted herb oil to make your salve.

You'll need:

A large bowl

About a square foot of cheesecloth

Rubber gloves

1 pound of cleaned beeswax (not paraffin wax)

A clean, old frying pan that you have designated for this use only

A wooden spoon you have designated for this use only

A ladle you have designated for this purpose only

Sterilized small jars (like jelly jars)

A cookie sheet lined with aluminum foil

To make your salve:

1. Strain the herb oil into the bowl through the cheesecloth. Wearing rubber gloves, squeeze the oil out of the cheesecloth. You can compost the discarded plant material.

2. Over very low heat, begin to melt about half the beeswax in the frying pan.

3. When the beeswax is liquid, begin to slowly and carefully pour oil from the bowl into the pan. If you have a quart of plant-infused oil, start with about one-third of the oil you have and gradually work upward as in the next step. (At this point, if you want to combine oils, you may do so. I like to combine comfrey and oregano for skin soothing and antimicrobial properties. I also add in a little eucalyptus essential oil.)

4. Stir carefully with the wooden spoon until the oils and the wax are completely combined. The mixture should look a little sludgy.

5. Using the wooden spoon, drop a few drops of the liquid mixture onto your aluminum foil–covered cookie sheet. Wait about two minutes for it to cool and then test the consistency with your fingers. If it feels like a good salve consistency, you're home free. If not, add a little more beeswax to make it harder or a little more oil to make it softer. You'll have to experiment a bit until you are satisfied.

6. Carefully pour the oil and beeswax mixture in your jars. Allow them to cool for an hour or two. If you wish, you can lightly cover them with a piece of cheesecloth.

7. Once the salve has set, cover, label, and date the jars. Store them in a cool, dark place. Salves are usually good for three to four years. If you open a jar and there's an "off" smell, discard the contents.

Note: Be a stickler about labeling your tinctures, salves, and dried herbs. Virtually all plant materials become unrecognizable when they are tinctured, dried, or placed in oils, so don't ever rely on your memory or your nose. Remember that your herbal tinctures and salves are true medicinals and, like any other medicines, they can be harmful if used incorrectly or in the wrong amounts.

You'll also notice that I included the botanical names with each plant listed in this chapter. That's because some plants are commonly known by other "nicknames," and I want to be sure we are talking about the same plants. This is particularly important if you are using them as medicinals. I can't stress enough that these are true medicinals with real effects. Like any other medicine, they should not be used carelessly.

CHAPTER 7

Growing Your Fruit

Growing fruit can be a hit-or-miss proposition; there are many variables to take into account. At my house we have luscious blackberries and a few stray blueberries here and there. My lone surviving apple tree is pathetic, but strawberries are another story entirely. (More on them in a bit. . . .)

Most fruits are perennials, the notable exceptions being highly nutritious melons. I love cantaloupes and watermelons, but I can't ever seem to get them beyond the softball-sized stage. I have better luck with the bush-type fruits, blackberries, raspberries, blueberries, and grapes.

Then finally, there are the fruit trees: apple, peach, pear, plum, cherry, and so forth. With many options and newer small-sized trees, you can grow a steady fruit supply for as long as fifty years with your own trees. Best of all, these fruit trees will grow in the widely varied climates throughout most of North America.

We'll start out with some generalities and then move on to the specifics of various types of fruit.

Planting in Pairs

The biggest generality is that almost all types of fruit need mates. In order for a tree, bush, or vining plant to bear fruit, its flowers must cross-pollinate, usually with a different variety of the same species. There are some self-pollinating fruit trees. Almost all citrus fruit trees are self-pollinating, as are most sour cherry, quince, and persimmon trees. However, the more common fruit trees and bushes will require another variety to be planted close by for pollination. The notable exception is the Golden Delicious apple, which is self-pollinating.

Be sure to carefully check the description of the tree you are planting. There's nothing more frustrating than planting a lovely tree and nurturing it to adulthood, watching it blossom gloriously in the spring, and then never reaping any fruit. In that case, lack of a mate has left your poor tree barren. If you want to cooperate with neighbors in providing mates, that will work fine, since pollination can take place as far away as several hundred yards.

Bees are an important element in the pollination process, which is why you don't want to use insecticides on your trees and plants. If you're not seeing bees in the vicinity of your trees and bushes, plant a few marigolds, cosmos, bee balm, or poppies near your trees to attract them there.

Where to Get Your Plants

Yes, it is possible to grow fruit trees and bushes from seeds. Didn't Johnny Appleseed plant his wares throughout the Midwest? But it is a slow process, and it is likely your new tree won't "run true" to the original.

It's easier and more reliable to buy your fruit trees and bushes from your local garden center or from a reliable mail-order supplier. There are many good ones, and you can be assured that if you are sold stock labeled as Gala apple, for example, that's what you will get. Growers also pretreat their stock for diseases.

If you buy your trees and bushes from a nursery, the label will usually tell you the age of the stock. Usually it will say "2- to 3-year-old trees," although sometimes the label will say "3- to 4-foot trees." Depending on the variety, you can expect to wait two or more years to get fruit when you buy the larger trees or bushes. If you've started from seed, it will probably be three or four years or more before you'll get fruit.

Many experts recommend buying bare-root trees and bushes because potted ones may be potbound and either be stunted or require time to recover. My personal experience has been that it doesn't matter, and potted trees and bushes have been just as healthy as bare-root. However, bare-root stock is usually less expensive, and if you're ordering from a mail-order nursery, shipping will be substantially cheaper.

Size

You may have reasons for wanting to grow full-sized fruit trees, but the newer dwarf trees are generally preferable because they take less space and you can usually harvest the fruit from the ground. For example, a dwarf apple tree will reach about 10 feet maximum height at full maturity, with a width of about 8 feet, while the fruit is normal size.

In general, dwarf trees bear fruit in fewer years than do standard-sized trees, but they usually bear less fruit. In my experience, some dwarf trees can bear so much fruit that it has to be culled to prevent the branches from breaking under the weight.

Dwarf trees are grafted from a dwarf root stock and a scion (upper part of the tree) that determines the fruiting variety, such as Red Delicious or Winesap or Granny Smith in the apple family.

You can even grow dwarf trees in containers, although you'll need to be prepared to pamper them a bit since they will need more pruning, watering, and soil amendment than trees grown in the ground. Pampering notwithstanding, I love the idea of growing an apple tree on a rooftop in Manhattan or an orange tree on a Miami terrace. All dwarf trees need to be pruned annually in order to maintain their size and shape. Unpruned dwarf trees will quickly become ungainly and too tall for harvesting from the ground.

Planting

My favorite gardening teacher once told me, "Dig a $25 hole for a $5 tree."

Translation: Put five times the effort into your planting as you do into the selection of your tree.

When you select your site, be sure it is in a good sunny location. All fruit trees need sun; at least six hours a day of direct sunlight. Next, check your soil. If your soil is hard as a rock or so sandy it doesn't hold together at all, you've got a job ahead of you to amend the soil so it is fertile and hospitable to your new little tree. If your soil is less than optimal, I suggest digging a big hole (3' x 3' wide by at least 3 feet deep) and mixing the existing soil with equal parts of well-rotted manure and compost.

If your soil is good and friable (you can squeeze together a clump in your hand and it separates into marble-sized pieces), you're good to go with a hole that is half again as deep and half again as wide as the nursery container of the tree you're planting. For example, if your tree is in a pot that is a foot wide and 16 inches deep, you'll need a hole that is 18 inches wide and 24 inches deep. If you have bare-root stock, dig your hole extravagantly, deep enough to leave plenty of room for all the roots to be fully extended vertically and wide enough for any braches that might be spread out.

Now check the drainage by pouring in enough water to fill the hole. Leave it for ten minutes. If all the water hasn't drained ("perked") from the hole in that time, you might want to reconsider your location. At the very least, poor drainage means you need to dig a bigger hole, fill it with more organic materials like well-rotted manure and compost, and perhaps add some gravel in the bottom of the hole to ensure that the roots won't rot from being too wet.

Trim your tree of any dead or unhealthy-looking branches or roots before you plant. If you're planting bare-root trees (available only in the dormant season), be sure to soak the roots in a bucket for an hour or two before planting. If you have a potted tree, be sure it is well watered, then remove the pot and check the roots carefully. Any roots that are swirled around the pot mean that it is root bound and you'll need to gently tease the roots into a straighter position.

Now you're ready to plant. Make a mound of soil in the bottom of the hole and gently place the new tree on top of the mound, carefully spreading the roots out like the rays of the sun.

Begin to shovel soil back into your hole, gently pressing it down as you go to ensure there are no air pockets around the roots. Your tree should be planted at exactly the same depth as it was in the pot. For bare-root trees, set your roots at ground level.

For grafted trees, be sure the bud union (it'll be an obvious knob where the root stock is grafted to the upper stock) is 2 inches above the soil line.

If you plan to stake your tree (recommended in most cases), pound the stake in the hole before you replace the soil to avoid damaging the roots later. Mulch around the base of the tree to control weeds and help retain water, taking care not to let the much layer touch the trunk of the tree, where excess moisture could cause rotting.

Use the same method for planting bushes or vines.

Be sure your plants get at least 1 inch of water a week for at least the first year, watering by hand if your rainfall is less than that.

Strawberries

Strawberries belong in a category of their own when it comes to fruit growing. I love them . . . and so do birds, so prepare to protect your berries with netting if you want any left for your own table.

You can easily grow strawberries in containers. A small garden patch in the full sun will give you a good yield. If you select June-bearing plants (the most popular because of their large, sweet fruit), you can expect many runners. Prune off all but 10 percent of the runners for the strongest plants and best yields. Everbearing and day-neutral strawberries will bear more than once a year and have few runners, but the fruit is smaller and not as sweet. Most strawberries are perennials, but a few varieties are biennials and will need to be replaced every other year. Once you have established a good strawberry bed, it will last for several years. During the first year, pinch off all the blossoms. You wont get any fruit, but you'll get strong heavy-bearing plants for years to come.

To avoid fungal diseases common in plants from the nightshade family, do not plant your vulnerable strawberries where tomatoes, potatoes, peppers, or eggplants have been grown in the past two years.

Protecting Your Fruit from Pests

Whether by insects, birds, or any or a variety of critters, your fruit crops are often in jeopardy of depredation. You can, however, grow fruit successfully and organically. It is not necessary to apply toxic sprays or take drastic measures.

Here are a few things to keep in mind:

1. Planting marigolds and other strong-scented flowers around the base of a bush or tree will repel many insects as well as rabbits and other animals that don't like the marigolds' spicy scent.

2. Attract beneficial insects to your garden. Some insects actually prey on others without damaging plants. This is why you should avoid using insecticides; they wipe out the good insects as well as the destructive ones. You want those ladybugs, lacewings, leaf miners, and trichogramma wasps, which eat destructive insects or feed on their eggs.

3. Keep the weeds down. That will help keep insects in check.

4. Fence young trees to keep hungry critters from chewing the bark. If their gnawings completely encircles the tree or bush—this is called "girdling"—it's an inevitable tree killer.

5. Use bird netting on bushes, berries, and small trees to keep birds away.

6. Try planting a mulberry tree to distract birds. Legend has it that mulberries are birds' hands-down favorite berries, so if you plant one nearby, they'll focus on it rather than on your blackberries or blueberries.

7. Urine: Deer and other unwelcome critters don't like the scent of predator urine. Garden catalogs will sell you elaborately packaged (and expensive) bobcat or coyote urine. Human urine is much more available and, best of all, it's free. If you have male family members, especially the younger ones who would delight in such activities, you can encourage them to sprinkle the perimeter from time to time. You'll need to renew the boundary frequently.

8. Scarecrows are a highly effective old-fashioned bird and critter repellant. You can also string old CDs throughout your garden for a sparkly deterrent or, if you want to get really fancy, try that Mylar-type ribbon or some whirligigs.

9. Motion sensor: If you're high-tech in nature, you can install a motion detector that will trigger a recording, perhaps of you yelling or some really loud music or, my favorite, one that trips a sprinkler and hoses down the intruders. Get creative when it comes to protecting your fruit!

CHAPTER 8

Preserving Your Harvest

Now that you're celebrating the success of your garden and patting yourself on the back and celebrating your bountiful harvest, you're probably thinking of resting on your laurels.

Not so fast!

What are you going to do with all that wonderful, glorious food?

After all, there is a limit to the number of tomatoes, peppers, cukes, zukes, and all the other produce that you can stuff in your face. And maybe, just maybe, you'd like to spread all that supernutrition over the coming months.

Never fear. There are lots of ways you can preserve your bounty simply and safely, and even have some fun in the bargain.

Canning

For me, canning is just too much trouble when I have maybe 10 pounds of tomatoes to process. I drag out all the equipment, make a total wreck of my kitchen, and end up with maybe 4 quart jars of tomatoes, only to start the whole mess all over the following week with 10 or 15 more pounds.

That's just the way of the garden: you've got a modest harvest of tomatoes or berries at any given time.

But canning is still a very worthwhile method of food preservation. It's energy efficient and requires minimal electricity or gas to process jars that can be sealed literally for decades.

Just as Grandma discovered during the Depression, canning saves money and creates healthier food choices in the home. If you're nervous about canning food, the processes used today are very safe when you follow the directions carefully.

Water-Bath Canner or Pressure Canner?

The most important piece of equipment for your canning adventures is the canner itself, but a lot of people don't know what type of canner to get or when to use pressure canning versus water-bath canning. The simple rule of thumb is that all high-acid foods go into a water-bath canner and everything else must be processed in a pressure canner.

High-acid foods are all fruit products (jams, jellies, preserves, conserves, fruit butters, and marmalades), tomatoes, tomato-based sauces and salsas, and anything pickled with vinegar, like pickles, relishes, and vinegar-based sauces. The hot-water bath increases the temperature in the canning jar enough to kill bacteria, and it also pushes out air bubbles as the content expands. As the jars cool, the air pressure makes the lid seal.

Low-acid foods are everything else: all nonpickled vegetables, meat, fish, poultry, and dried beans. The pressure cooker gets much hotter than a water-bath canner (250°F), and it maintains that heat throughout processing to kill microbes.

Buying Guide

Water-bath canners are made of aluminum or porcelain-covered steel. They have removable perforated racks and fitted lids. The canner must be deep enough so that at least 1 inch of briskly boiling water will be over the tops of jars during processing. Some water-bath canners do not have a flat bottom, which is the only kind that will work on an electric stove. Either a flat or ridged bottom can be used on a gas burner. To ensure uniform processing of all jars with an electric range, the diameter of the canner should be no more than 4 inches wider than the burner element on which it is heated.

You need a water-bath canner that is deep enough to submerge your jars. Look for one that has a rack for the jars so they don't clank together during boiling. Some home preservers use a large stockpot and homemade rack system, but you can find very affordable water-bath canning kits for under $30.

By comparison, home-use pressure canners have been extensively redesigned in recent years. Models made before the '70s were heavy-walled kettles with clamp-on or turn-on lids, fitted with a dial gauge, a vent port in the form of a petcock or counterweight, and a safety fuse. Modern pressure canners are lightweight, thin-walled kettles; most have turn-on lids. They have a jar rack, a gasket, a dial or weighted gauge, an automatic vent/cover lock, a vent port (steam vent) to be closed with a counterweight or weighted gauge, and a safety fuse.

A pressure canner runs about $100 for a 10- to 16-quart size. However, a pressure canner easily becomes a water-bath canner just by leaving the lid off. It can also be used for other culinary efforts, such as tenderizing inexpensive cuts of meat. If you're planning to do a lot of canning or doing more than jam and pickles, get a pressure canner; it offers more options.

Tools of the Trade

The following is a list of the basic equipment a home canner will need to operate. Now is the time to take an inventory of your canning supplies and equipment and start gathering screwbands (also called rings), lids, and jars. The jars and screwbands are reusable, but to ensure a good seal, you must use new lids for every batch. The lids are readily available at most supermarkets.

If your pressure canner uses a rubber gasket, get a pair of them. If a gasket blows in the middle of a canning project, you'll need the replacement right at your fingertips.

Check out your local thrift shops and see if you can get a supply of Mason jars cheap. You may have to ask, because they don't always put jars on display. Also post a note on your local Freecycle network (*www.freecycle.org*); sometimes you can get canning equipment, and all it costs is the gas to go pick it up. Just be absolutely sure the rims of used jars are free of nicks, cracks, and chips that could allow in contaminants.

BASIC CANNING EQUIPMENT

- One or more canning books with recipes
- Water-bath canner (You can use a large stockpot with a lid. Any pot used as a water-bath canner must have a rack to keep the jars off the bottom.)

- Pressure canner if you intend to put up vegetables, meats, and nonacidic products
- Canning jars—pints, quarts, and jelly-size Mason jars
- Lids and rings
- Large spoons for mixing and stirring
- Metal soup ladles
- Sharp paring knives
- Veggie peelers
- Canning funnel
- Colander and/or large strainer
- Large slotted spoons
- Measuring cups and spoons
- Squeezer or juicer
- Food mill, food processor, and/or blender
- Canning-jar lifter and lid wand
- Stirrer for getting air bubbles out of jars
- Kitchen timer
- Cheesecloth for making spice balls or large tea balls
- Pickling or canning salt, Fruit-Fresh, powdered and liquid pectin, and Clear Jel A
- Kitchen towels
- Aprons
- Disposable rubber gloves
- Long-handled jar scrubber
- Kitchen scale (optional)
- Jelly bags (optional)
- Zester, mandolin, melon baller, apple peeler, or cherry pitter (optional)

Jars, Lids, and Screwbands

Only jars specifically designated as canning jars are safe for canning. Commercial jars like those for mayonnaise and peanut butter were designed for one-time use only. They may crack or shatter in either a water-bath or a pressure canner. Those lovely antique jars with the old bail-wire lids look pretty, but they are no longer recommended for canning. Save the antique jars for storage purposes.

Use canning jars in sizes suitable for the product and your family's needs. Canning jars generally are sold in half-pint, pint, and quart sizes with wide and regular mouths. Wide-mouth jars are convenient for packing such foods as whole tomatoes and peach halves. Quart jars are convenient for vegetables and fruits if your family has four or more members.

Some commercial pasta sauces are packaged in canning-type jars. Note, however, that they are not a full quart. Also, make absolutely certain that the screwband fits it perfectly, as some threading on these jars does not match that of the commercially available screwbands.

If you have extra unused lids, store them protected in a dry, cool place. A Rubbermaid storage box with a tight-fitting lid works quite well for storage of extra lids and screwbands.

Before storing used screwbands, wash them in hot soapy water and dry them well.

Preparation

Before you start canning, read the recipe at least twice and get your ingredients together. Organize the supplies and equipment you will need to complete your project. Learning you are out of a certain ingredient in the middle of a canning session is not fun!

Also remember: Canning projects require your uninterrupted attention from start to finish. Turn off your cell phone and just get into the Zen of it. You'll find there is a certain joy in having tomato juice dripping off your elbows.

Next, prepare your workspace. Arrange the kitchen counters so you have ample space to work. Examine the jars carefully, making certain there are no cracks or chips. You may put them through a sterilizing cycle in a dishwasher if you have one. Otherwise, use a bottle brush to scrub them inside and out, rinse them in hot water, and sterilize them by dipping them in boiling water for a few seconds. Meanwhile, place the lids in a bowl of hot water to soften the rubber sealing compound.

When you're filling jars, cushion them with an old folded terrycloth bath towel folded in half. Never put jars on an uncovered countertop since they could crack or worse yet, crack your countertop when you fill the jars with hot foods.

Remember to leave the proper amount of headspace in the jars for expansion—¼ inch for jams, jellies, preserves, and most other water-bath processed foods, and 1 inch for pressure-processed foods. Each recipe will specify the amount of headspace. Too little headspace may cause liquid to seep out; too much headspace and food at the top of the jar may dry out.

Finally, remove air bubbles from the jar. This can be accomplished by gently stirring the contents of the jar. A chopstick works great. Use a damp kitchen towel to wipe the outer rims, then put on a lid and screw the band firmly. Do not overtighten screwbands. Doing so may cause lids to buckle in the canner.

Processing

In a water-bath canner, jars are placed on a rack and covered by 1 to 2 inches of boiling water. Put a lid on the canner and begin timing when water is boiling. Remove jars with a jar lifter and place them on a towel-covered counter to cool. Leave undisturbed for 12 to 24 hours. Check the seals and remove the screwbands.

In a pressure canner, jars are placed on a rack and boiling water is added according to the manufacturers' instructions. Lock the lid securely into place. Leave weight off the vent pipe or open petcock and exhaust steam for 10 minutes. Place weight back onto vent pipe or close petcock. Canner should start to pressurize in 5–10 minutes. Once the canner has reached the required amount of pressure, start the timer. Allow canner to come down to zero pounds on its own. Do not try to speed up this process by removing weight or opening the petcock, as it may cause jars to crack and/or lose liquid. Do not put the canner into cold water to hasten the process. Let jars sit in the canner for 5–10 minutes to allow them to cool down. Remove jars with a jar lifter and place them on a towel-covered counter to cool. Leave undisturbed for 12 to 24 hours. Check the seals and remove the screwbands.

To check the seals on cooled jars, press your thumb in the middle of the lid. If the lid seems to give and come back up, the jar isn't sealed. If you're not sure, tap the lid with a knife in the same place. It should sound like a bell; a muffled sound means the jar isn't sealed right. Finally, there's the visual: The surface of the lid should be concave.

What happens if your jar doesn't seal properly? All is not lost! You have several options here. One is to put the jar in the refrigerator and use it soon. Second is to try reprocessing the jar within twenty-four hours of the original effort. If you're going to do this, open the jar, make sure the lid has a clean surface, try changing out the lid, and put everything back in your canner. Your third and fourth options are using other preservation methods covered in this book, namely freezing or drying, if practicable.

After Processing

Wash off all of the sealed jars, label them with the contents and the date of canning, and move them into a suitable storage place. To prevent spoiling, keep the jars away from places that are too hot or damp, and don't expose them to bright light. Use your canned goods within one year unless otherwise specified by the recipe.

When you use your canned goods, always check for signs of spoilage. The most obvious sign is the loss of a vacuum seal on the jar and mold growing inside. Other indicators include gas bubbles, odd coloring, and foul smells. Never test suspect food—throw it out!

Safe Temperatures for Canning

At sea level, water boils at 212ºF. This is the processing temperature for all high-acid and pickled foods. It is the temperature at which molds, yeasts, and some bacteria are destroyed.

Low-acid, nonpickled foods are processed in a pressure canner at 250ºF. It is the temperature at which bacterial spores (botulinum) are destroyed. Botulism is odorless, colorless, and tasteless. In the case of an otherwise healthy adult, it mimics stomach flu symptoms. In the case of a small child, an elderly adult, or a person with an impaired immune system, it can be fatal.

Also pay close attention to the canning instructions given in your canning guide. Extensive instructions on safe home canning can be obtained from your county Cooperative Extension office or from the U.S. Department of Agriculture (*www.usda.gov*).

Foods containing pasta, rice, or barley cannot be canned safely. These low-acid ingredients, which are common to soups, stews, and other convenience meals, need to be pressure-processed at length. During this time they break down and may, in fact, make the foodstuff too dense for the heat to safely kill the botulism spores. Besides, who wants to eat overcooked pasta or rice? Yuck.

Second, dairy products, including eggs, milk, cream, cheese, and butter, are not safe to can. You can make pickled eggs and refrigerate them, but they need to be used within two weeks.

Oils aren't good candidates either. While flavored oils can be made for short-term use, oils generally get rancid very quickly.

Anything heavy in fats doesn't can well. Excess fat should be removed from meat, and ground beef should be sautéed and drained of excess fat. Allow soups and stocks to cool, skim off the fat, and then reheat and process them. Like oils, fat tends to go rancid.

Last but not least, don't can anything thickened with flour, cornstarch, arrowroot, or bread crumbs. Clear Jel A, which is a modified cornstarch, may be used for safely canning pie fillings but is not safe for thickening sauces or gravies.

Finally, have fun! While the rules sound like drudgery, they're really not difficult. I like to invite a friend or two to can with me. We might drink a little wine, laugh a lot, and when all is said and done, we have only one kitchen to clean up.

Freezing Your Harvest

Freezing is almost the easiest way to preserve foods, but it's not terribly energy-efficient since it requires a substantial amount of electricity to keep your produce from spoiling and you can lose everything during a power failure.

Freezing comes close to totally stopping microbial development because the water in frozen food turns to ice, in which bacteria cannot continue to grow. Enzyme activity, on the other hand, isn't completely deterred by freezing, which is why many vegetables are blanched before being packaged so they won't turn brown and become mushy. Once an item is defrosted completely, however, any microbes still within will begin to grow again.

What Can Be Frozen?

Except for eggs in the shell, nearly all foods can be frozen raw or after blanching or cooking. So the real question here is what foods don't take well to freezing. Not to worry. Virtually everything form your garden will freeze beautifully.

If you're ever in doubt about how to best prepare an item for freezing (or even whether you should freeze it), the National Center for Home Preserving (*www.uga.edu/nchfp*) is a great online resource. It offers tips on how to freeze various items ranging from pie and prepared food to oysters and artichokes.

Strive to keep your freezer temperature at 0°F (18°C) for optimal texture and taste. Before buying a freezer, check to see that it achieves that temperature, if not colder.

A freezer thermometer will assure you that you've got your temperature where you want it.

Equipment

Once you're ready to begin, assemble all the items you need. For example, if you're freezing fruit, you'll want a clean cutting board, a sharp knife, and your choice of storage containers. If you're doing any preparation of the fruit before freezing it, you'll also need cooking pans. Stainless steel is highly recommended; galvanized pans may give off zinc when fruit is left in them because of the fruit's acid content. Additionally, there's nothing like stainless steel for easy cleanup.

If it's in your budget, a vacuum sealer is another great piece of equipment. Vacuum sealers come in a variety of sizes with a similar variety of bags that are perfect for preservers who like freezing and drying methods. They're fairly cost-effective when compared to freezer bags or plastic containers, and they eliminate the excess air that contributes to the buildup of ice crystals and the deterioration of quality.

A third item that you shouldn't be without is a freezer-proof labeling system. If you double-wrap your frozen items, put a label on each layer. If one gets knocked off, the other remains.

Vegetables

Vegetables should be chosen for crispness and freshness. If you're preserving food from your garden, pick it within a few hours before packing.

The next step for vegetables is blanching or briefly dipping produce in boiling water and then plunging them into an ice-water bath to stop the cooking. Blanching also removes the peels of soft fruits like tomatoes and peaches. In addition, it can be used to partially cook vegetables like beans or peas so they retain their crunch when frozen. Blanching will improve the lifespan of your frozen goods.

If there's no specific blanching time provided in your preserving recipe, here's a brief overview to get you started. Remember to move the vegetables into an ice-water bath immediately after blanching and leave them there until they're totally cooled

> **TIP**
> When freezing beans or peas or blueberries or blackberries—anything that is not too squishy—spread the goods in a single layer on a cookie sheet and put them uncovered in the freezer just until they are frozen solid, usually not more than a couple of hours. Then load them into freezer bags, label, and pop them into the freezer before they have a chance to thaw. This way, the contents are loose and you can take out a handful whenever you like without defrosting the entire bag.

TIMING AND TECHNIQUES FOR BLANCHING VEGETABLES

- **Asparagus.** Remove the tough ends from the asparagus. Depending on the storage container, you may need to cut the stems in half. If your stalks are thin, they'll only need 2 minutes of blanching; thick stalks require twice as much.
- **Beans (green or wax).** Remove any tips. Leave the beans whole and blanch them for 3 minutes.
- **Brussels sprouts.** Clean off outer leaves, then soak the sprouts in cold salt water for 30 minutes. Drain and blanch for 4 minutes.
- **Cabbage.** Remove the outer leaves. Shred the cabbage and blanch for 1 minute. Leave the cabbage in the water for another 30 seconds before icing.
- **Carrots.** Clean the skins, then slice the carrots into ¼" pieces. Blanch for 3 minutes. Whole baby carrots need 5 minutes of blanching.
- **Cauliflower and broccoli.** Break off the pieces from the central core and clean well (a spray nozzle at the sink works very well). Soak in a gallon of saltwater (3–4 teaspoons salt per gallon) for 30 minutes. Pour off the saltwater. Rinse and blanch for 3 minutes
- **Corn.** Rinse, remove from the cob, and blanch for 5 minutes.
- **Mushrooms (small).** These can be frozen whole. Toss with a little fresh lemon juice and blanch for 4 minutes.
- **Greens (including spinach).** Rinse. Remove any leaves that have spots or other damage. Blanch for 3 minutes.
- **Peas (shelled).** Blanch for 90 seconds.
- **Peas in the pod.** Trim the ends and remove strings. Blanch for 1–2 minutes, depending on the size of the pod.
- **Peppers.** Slice open and remove the seeds. Cut into desired size and blanch for 2 minutes.
- **Potatoes.** Wash and scrub thoroughly. Remove the peel and blanch for 4 minutes.

- **Tomatoes.** To easily peel the skins, use a straining spoon and dip the tomatoes in boiling water for 30 seconds. Peel and remove the core. These can be stored whole or diced to desired size.
- **Zucchini and squash.** Peel. Cut into ½-inch slices and blanch for 3 minutes.

Fruit

Prepare small batches of fruit so it doesn't brown while you're packing. Fruit need not be packed in syrup, but many people do prefer the texture and taste that sugar or sugar syrup adds to frozen fruit. Some folks use sugar substitutes like Splenda for dietary reasons. In any case, berries take well to a simple sprinkling. Larger chunks such as peaches do well in syrup. The average ratio is ½ cup of syrup to every pint of fruit. Note that some preservers like to use ascorbic acid to improve the quality of frozen fruit. Adding about ½ teaspoon of this per pint is sufficient; just mix it into the syrup or a little water.

Packaging

Since 95 percent of American homes freeze some of their food regularly, it's not surprising to find that people have a lot of questions on the best type of storage containers to use and how to prepare food for the table after it's been frozen. Plastic bags designed to hold frozen foods (not storage bags) are the most common receptacles, followed by plastic containers.

Overall, it's always a good idea to use bags and containers that are rated for freezing.

Your packaging materials should also be leak and oil resistant, and all packing materials should be able to withstand freezing.

Space Constraints

When you're packing food into a container, always leave a little room for expansion. Let the food reach room temperature before you freeze it (right out of the ice-water bath is a perfect time with vegetables). Putting warm or hot food in the freezer creates a temperature variance for all the food inside the freezer.

Most important, remember to label and date everything. This will help you gauge what should be eaten first so it retains the greatest quality.

Safe Storage Times

Frozen food can be kept nearly indefinitely at 0°F or colder. Nonetheless, the longer the food stays frozen, the more nutrients you lose and the greater the likelihood that ice crystals will form and decrease the overall color, taste, or textural quality of the product. One great way to deter this is by simple rotation. Diligently arrange your freezer shelves so that the oldest items are in front and newly preserved items are in the back.

Defrosting

Many people have questions about how to safely defrost food. The first rule of defrosting is that you don't leave anything at room temperature for hours at a time. Instead, there are two tried-and-true ways to safely defrost your food.

- Transfer the food from the freezer to the refrigerator and leave it there. This method takes a while, and it's wise to put some paper towels or a platter underneath the item to catch any water or juices that run out during defrosting.
- Put the food in a cold-water bath. Keep the item in the wrapper or container, and if need be put it in an additional resealable bag for protection. It's recommended that you refresh the water every 30 minutes until the item is defrosted.

Using the refrigerator is the recommended approach that seems to best protect the overall quality of the food. Note that about 1 pound of food takes about a day to defrost this way, so plan accordingly.

Refreezing

The beauty of thawing food in your refrigerator is that you can refreeze it quite safely, as long as it's kept properly cold. You might lose a little moisture with meat and bread products, texture with vegetables, and flavor with juices, but there's no issue with microbial growth because the average refrigerator keeps food at 30–48°F (30–40°F is ideal). Similarly, if you cook an item that was previously frozen, you can freeze any leftovers safely. Note, however, that some experts feel it's a good precaution to cook completely thawed meat before refreezing.

Partially defrosted food is a little different. If there are still ice crystals in the pack and the food has not been left at room temperature, it's relatively safe—just make sure there's no discoloration or odd odor. Any food that's been completely thawed to warm or room temperature should not be refrozen and should be discarded if it's been out longer than two hours.

> **HOW LONG WILL MY FOOD STAY FROZEN IF THERE'S A POWER OUTAGE?**
> If you leave your freezer closed, and it is in a cool part of the house (like your basement), food stays frozen up to four days in a well-stocked freezer. When the freezer is half full or less, food will start to thaw in twenty-four hours.

Drying

Drying was one of the first preserving methods ever used, probably because of its simplicity. Dehydrating foods as a means of preserving food is super-easy and energy efficient because dried food requires no electricity to store. Without water content, food doesn't spoil—dried tomatoes can last for years with virtually no attention—and it packs very neatly onto cupboard shelves. The low-heat dehydration process also preserves precious nutrients exceptionally well.

In addition, preserving food in this way can allow you to get creative in some truly strange ways (like the time I discovered that some zucchini too large to eat dried into "chips" that were very palatable and healthy when sprinkled with a little salt and pepper and dehydrated).

Methods of Drying

Unlike canning, drying is a little more alchemical than other preservation methods because of all the things that affect it. For example, temperature variations and humidity will both affect the drying process, specifically how long it will take. Pay attention to these things so that you can adjust your drying method accordingly. There are a variety of different ways to dry food.

> **TIP**
>
> When considering which drying method is best for you, don't forget to look at your environment. To sun-dry food, for example, you'll need about five days of low humidity and high temperatures (95°F being ideal). While someone in Arizona might use this method with no difficulty, it's not likely to be practical for, say, someone in New York in January.

Air

Herbs and flowers are the most common air-dried foods. If you grow your own, harvest herbs and flowers before 10 A.M. to retain the greatest amount of essential oil for aroma and flavor. The later hours in the day cause the oils to retreat into the plant stem (or dry up) from the heat of the sun. If you're hanging the plants, don't bundle more than about six stems together at once. Hang them upside down from a string in a dry, warm spot with a paper lunch bag draped loosely over the bundle to keep it free from dust and protect against sunlight. Use a toothpick to make holes in the bag to allow air to circulate.

An alternative method of drying is to remove the flower petals or herb leaves from the stem and lay them on a screen. It's very important that the screening material be clean and that the plant pieces don't touch each other. Again, this protects the flowers and herbs from airborne dust and dirt.

There's a wide variety of food that can be dried, including fish, fruit, edible flowers, meat, vegetables, and herbs. The taste and texture of dried food is different from fresh or frozen, so make small batches at first to see how well you like the results. Keep a list of items that you like best and return to those recipes to make larger batches later.

Oven-Drying

You can use your oven on low heat for many hours; however, the bottom line on your electric and/or gas bill may price this method right out of your comfort zone.

On the other hand, oven-drying is very simple. Get out oven trays, preheat your oven to 140ºF, and pre-prepare your food according to the instructions in the Drying Fruit and Drying Vegetables sections of this chapter. Most oven trays hold up to 2 pounds of food. Unless you have a very large oven, it's suggested that you dry no more than three trays at a time.

Oven-drying is pretty labor intensive. You need to shift the trays and turn the food every 30 minutes for best results. Finally, try to keep the door of the oven open about 2 inches throughout this time. This improves air circulation and decreases the amount of heat you lose when you circulate the drying items.

Food Dehydrator

Using a commercial electric dehydrator takes half the time as drying in an oven, making it perfect for the energy-conscious consumer. An additional benefit is that these devices are created specifically to maintain air circulation, sustain even heating, and safeguard nutritional value so they take little baby-sitting. Fruits, herbs, and meats are good candidates for the dehydrator.

The market for dehydrators has grown, which means you can find some great optional features—for a price. You can pay more than $300 for a stainless steel dehumidifier with 16 cubic feet of interior space, but most home preservers don't need anything quite so impressive. If you plan to spend between $60 and $75, you'll usually get a good-quality machine.

There are two basic types of dehydrators on the market. One dries the food using a fan and heat from the side; the other dries food from the bottom of the machine. I have two dehydrators, one with the side fan and one from the bottom. I think both work equally well. Some say the round bottom-fan dehydrators don't dry as evenly, but I have not found that to be true.

Watch for machine features that will make your life easier. For example, a temperature gauge lets you adjust the heat to specific food groups, allowing you to produce a higher-quality dried item. Additionally, you want a dehydrator that fits in your kitchen comfortably and has enough trays to make several layers of dried goods, a timer to keep things from overcooking, and a good warranty. Last but not least, dishwasher-safe parts save you a lot of time.

For Drying Success: Freshness, Attentiveness, and Airflow

In drying, "fresh is best" is your mantra. The sooner you begin drying items after they've been harvested, the happier you'll be with the results. This is also one of the few times in cooking when you'll hear "faster is better." When you carefully and quickly dry goods, it helps give you better texture and ensures that you don't have any moisture in the center of each piece of food. Nonetheless, most drying techniques do take some time.

I tend to run my dehydrators 24/7 in August and September. Of course, foods dry more quickly if they are sliced razor thin, but they also have less flavor, in my opinion. In general, you can expect tomatoes to take about 12 to14 hours to dry, depending on the humidity of the day. That means if you start a batch early in the morning, you can have the next batch in by mid-evening and keep that cycle going pretty much indefinitely.

Drying Fruit

Bargains are great, but when you're drying foods, you want the freshest and most unblemished pieces you can find. Remember Garbage In, Garbage Out? Well, that applies to dehydrating food, too.

If you are buying foods to dehydrate, look for the closest to organic you can find, since toxic residues can remain on your foods, no matter how well they are washed.

Cleaning and Slicing

All fruit requires a good washing before you begin. With items like peaches or apples, you'll need to get rid of the core or pit. Peel the fruit before slicing it thinly. If you're drying something like grapes, treat the skins to a swim in boiling water. Use a strainer to dunk them in a bowl of cold water, then lay them aside to dry. This method is called "cracking," and it lets air into the fruit for better drying.

Battling Browning

Once sliced, almost all fruit begins to brown fairly quickly. Keeping the browning to a minimum improves the overall quality of your dried fruit because it does impact the overall quality of dried fruit. The easiest way of preventing oxidation is to toss the sliced fruit in an ascorbic acid (vitamin C) bath once it's cut (1 teaspoon dissolved in 1 cup of water for 5 quarts of soft fruit like peaches; 2 teaspoons for hard fruit like apples).

While most of us think of tomatoes as vegetables, they are actually fruit. Tomatoes dry very well and may have a leathery texture when the drying process is complete.

Budget about 6 to 12 hours to completely dry fruit pieces. Smaller slices or pieces dry the fastest. Always cut open a piece and check the interior to make sure the process is complete.

Drying Vegetables

Not all vegetables take well to drying. When you start thinking about drying vegetables, consider which ones have the shortest shelf life and which of those might be better suited to freezing. For example, the texture of asparagus doesn't translate well with drying and dehydration, so this is one vegetable you may want to freeze instead.

Your vegetables should be fully grown and in peak condition. If you can harvest them from your garden, that's fantastic. However, don't buy or harvest more than you want for drying in one batch. This keeps your kitchen space more manageable. Thoroughly clean and cut the vegetables to the desired size, remembering that the larger the piece, the longer the drying time.

Some vegetable parts, such as celery leaf, dry quickly; other parts will take as long as comparable fruit pieces. Dried vegetables are hard and crunchy. It's recommended that you store each type of vegetable separately in airtight, carefully labeled containers. Keep them away from sunlight or heat for the greatest longevity.

Conclusion: A Rewarding Task Results in a Healthy Lifestyle

At the beginning of this book, I set out to give you the secrets of health and long life with foods you can grow. I hope you've gained some valuable insight into the myriad ways the foods you eat—and the foods you grow right in your own backyard or on your own deck or windowsill—will not only keep you healthy but address your health complaints.

Whether you're treating insect bites, sunburn, and canker sores, or cancer, heart disease, diabetes, and everything in between, the food you eat is the foundation of your health and your recovery.

Yes, supplements can be helpful. Yes, sometimes you need medical attention and all the power that modern medicine and prescription drugs can offer. I always remember Dr. Andrew Weil's comment: "If I'm in a car accident, don't take me to an herbalist!" Still, the foods you eat and the nutritional status you've established will unquestionably have great influence on the outcome of your health challenges.

For most of us, most of the time, the foods we can grow in our own gardens or buy close to where they were grown are our greatest allies in wellness, our most powerful preventive tools, our most potent curatives, and the source of great joy.

Hopefully, armed with helpful info, you're inspired to start a garden or get out into your already-established garden, feel the sun on your shoulders, and savor the freshest food on earth. As I write this, I am snacking on a dozen cherry tomatoes picked from my garden ten minutes ago. What a gift!

I'd like to hear your health and gardening experiences. Please visit my website, *www.kathleenbarnes.com*, to offer comments and complaints, or e-mail me directly at *Kathleen@kathleenbarnes.com*.

Resources

Books

Abbott, Catherine, *The Everything® Grow Your Own Vegetables Book.* (Avon, MA: Adams Media, 2010).

Bartholomew, Mel, *All New Square Foot Gardening: Grow More in Less Space!* (Nashville, TN: Cool Springs Press, 2006).

Duke, James, *The Green Pharmacy Guide to Healing Foods.* (Emmaus, PA: Rodale, 2008).

Lavelle, Christine and Michael, *How to Grow Organic Vegetables, Fruit, Herbs, Flowers.* (London: Southwater, 2008).

Pratt, Steven, and Matthews, Kathy, *Superfoods RX* (New York: William Morrow, 2004).

Telesco, Patricia, and Maack, Jeanne P., *The Everything® Canning and Preserving Book* (Avon, MA: Adams Media, 2009).

Yeager, Selene, and the Editors of Prevention Health Books, *Prevention's New Foods for Healing* (Emmaus, PA: Rodale, 1998).

Websites

WebMd
www.webmd.com

Natural Cure
www.naturalcures.com

The Cancer Cure Foundation
www.cancure.org

Natural Health News
www.naturalnews.com

Dr. Hyla Cass
www.cassmd.com

Pharmacist Suzy Cohen
www.dearpharmacist.com

Dr. James Duke
www.greenpharmacy.com

Chris Kilham, The Medicine Hunter
www.medicinehunter.com

Dr. Joe Mercola
www.mercola.com

Dr. Ray Sahelian
www.raysahelian.com

Dr. Jacob Teitelbaum
www.endfatigue.com

Dr. Andrew Weil
www.drweil.com

Gardens Alive! (source for nontoxic pesticides, herbicides, and fertilizers and great resource for pest control and disease identification information)
www.gardensalive.com

Spray-N-Grow natural fertilizers
www.spray-n-grow.com

INDEX

About the Author

Kathleen Barnes is an ardent advocate of natural health and an equally avid gardener. Her career as a journalist and writer has spanned more than four decades, including years as an international correspondent for ABC and CNN during historic transitions in the Philippines and South Africa. In recent years, she has turned her writing to natural health and sustainable living, writing, and editing fifteen books.

She has written extensively for national and international publications, including more than six years as the weekly natural health columnist for *Woman's World* magazine.

Kathleen lives in the Blue Ridge Mountains of western North Carolina with her husband, Joe, and an ever-changing extended family of horses, dogs, cats, and the occasional pond frog.

Kathleen Barnes's other books include:

Eight Weeks to Vibrant Health: A Take Charge Plan for Women with Dr. Hyla Cass. (Brevard, NC: Take Charge Books, 2008 second edition, first edition McGraw-Hill).

The Calcium Lie: What Your Doctor Doesn't Know Might Kill You with Dr. Robert Thompson. (Brevard, NC: Take Charge Books, 2008).

The Secret of Health: Breast Wisdom with Dr. Ben Johnson. (Garden City, NY: Morgan James Publishing 2007).

User's Guide to Thyroid Disorders. (Laguna Beach, CA: Basic Health Publications, 2006).

User's Guide to Natural Hormone Replacement. (Laguna Beach, CA: Basic Health Publications, 2006).

Arthritis and Joint Health. (Orem, UT: Woodland Publishing, 2005).